THE JUNCTION

An aerial view of the Junction, where the Chilcotin and Fraser rivers come together. Photo courtesy of Earl Cahill and Don Logan.

THE JUNCTION

Stories of Land and Place in the BC Interior

JOHN SCHREIBER

CAITLIN PRESS

Caitlin Press Inc.
8100 Alderwood Road,
Halfmoon Bay, BC V0N 1Y1
www.caitlin-press.com

Text design by Kathleen Fraser.
Cover design by Vici Johnstone.
Cover photo courtesy of Larry Travis, Raincoast Images,
and Jane Woodland and Chris Genovali, Raincoast Conservation Foundation.
Edited by Audrey McClellan.
Printed in Canada.

Caitlin Press Inc. acknowledges financial support from the Government of Canada through the Canada Book Fund and the Canada Council for the Arts, and from the Province of British Columbia through the British Columbia Arts Council and the Book Publisher's Tax Credit.

Library and Archives Canada Cataloguing in Publication

Schreiber, John, 1941–, author
        The junction : stories of land and place in the BC interior / John Schreiber.

Includes bibliographical references.
ISBN 978-1-927575-21-5 (pbk.)

        1. Schreiber, John, 1941– —Travel—British Colmubia—Cariboo Region. 2. Cariboo Region (B.C.)—Description and travel—Anecdotes. 3. Cariboo Region (B.C.)—Social life and customs—21st century—Anecdotes. I. Title.

FC3845.C445S29 2013   917.11'75045   C2013-905671-8

In our thoughtworld, myth and reality are opposites. Unless we can find some way to understand the reality of mythic thinking, we will remain prisoners of our own language, our own thoughtworld. In this world one story is real, the other fantasy. In the Indian way of thinking both stories are true because they describe personal experience. Their truths are complementary.

—"Fox and Chickadee"
in *Little Bit Know Something*
Robin Ridington

From the Tibetan perspective, to go into the mountains blind, knowing nothing of proper ritual protocols, living in complete ignorance of anything but what lies on the surface of perception, was an act of complete folly. To enter the hidden lands of Khenbalung without adequate spiritual protection, as the British [mountaineers] were destined to do, would seem a sign of madness.

—Into the Silence
Wade Davis

CONTENTS

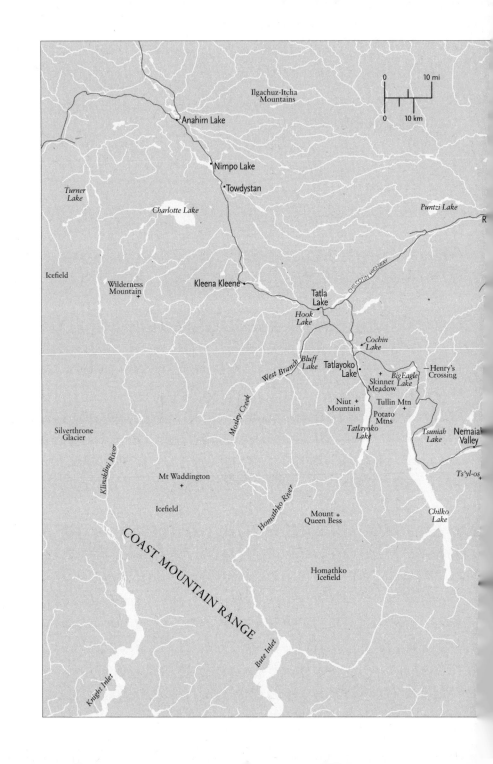

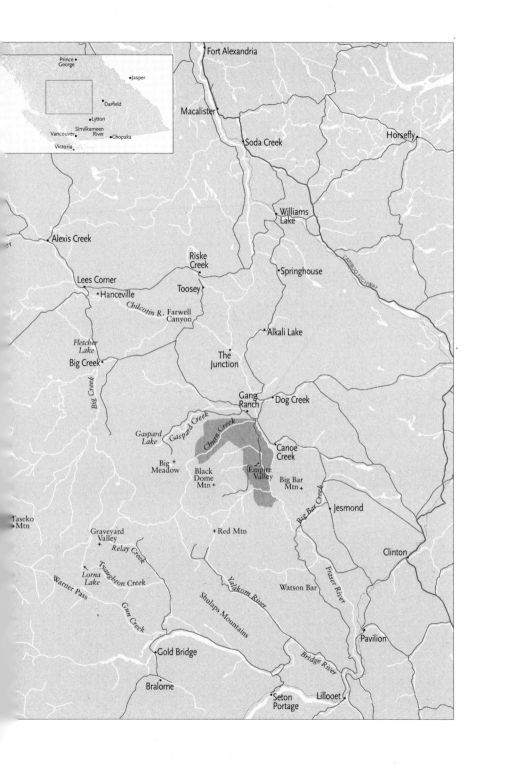

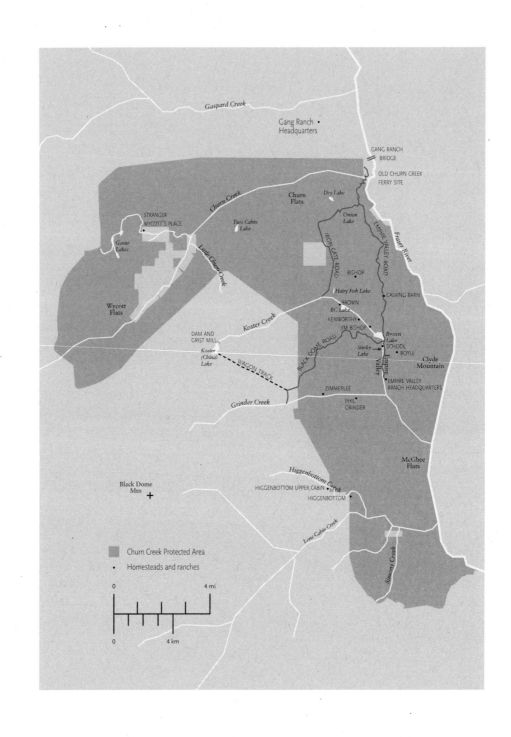

Gaspard Creek

Gang Ranch
Headquarters

GANG RANCH
BRIDGE

OLD CHURN CREEK
FERRY SITE

Churn Creek

Churn
Flats

Dry Lake

Onion
Lake

STRANGER
WYCOTT'S PLACE

Two Cabin
Lake

EMPIRE VALLEY ROAD

Fraser River

Goose
Lakes

Little Churn Creek

IRON GATE ROAD

BISHOP

Wycott
Flats

Koster Creek

Hairy Fish Lake

CALVING BARN

BROWN

B.C. Lake

KENWORTHY

DAM AND
GRIST MILL

JIM BISHOP

BLACK DOME ROAD

Brown
Lake

SCHOOL

BOYLE

Koster
(China)
Lake

WAGON TRACK

Stinky
Lake

Empire Valley

Clyde
Mountain

EMPIRE VALLEY
RANCH HEADQUARTERS

ZIMMERLEE

Grinder Creek

PHIL
GRINDER

McGhee
Flats

Black Dome
Mtn +

Higgenbottom Creek

HIGGENBOTTOM UPPER CABIN

HIGGENBOTTOM

Lone Cabin Creek

Simons Creek

■ Churn Creek Protected Area

• Homesteads and ranches

0   4 mi

0   4 km

INTRODUCTION
Passing through Writing-On-Stone

We shall not cease from exploration
And the end of all our exploring
Will be to arrive where we started
And know the place for the first time.
—T.S. Eliot, "Little Gidding"

THROUGHOUT MY LIFE I'VE BEEN FOCUSED ON PLACES: BRITISH COLUMBIAN places, Coast and Interior, Western Canadian places; the list of communities and cities where I've lived, however briefly in some cases, is long. They are mostly rural and range from Duncan, Vancouver, Port McNeill, Mahatta River, Moresby Camp and Victoria on the coast to Darfield, Mount Currie and Prince George inland, all in the southern half of this province. I could name a few more short stops: Jeune Landing, Holberg, Woodfibre, and Nitinat Camp on Cowichan Lake. The latter was named Camp Three when my family lived there for several months in 1943. Our front street consisted of steel railroad tracks spiked to wooden ties. I was only two years old, but my memories of our time there are powerful; certain events are sharp in my mind even now. To this day, the pungent smell of hedge nettle in spring (a Camp Three memory), wafting through my open car window, just about drives me off the road. A raven's croak hanging in still air, evocative of a breezeless, Cowichan blue-sky summer walk along the tracks with my mother, stops me cold.

There are places farther north that I've ventured to: places like Fort St. James, Grassy Plains, Hazelton, Kitwancool, Fort St. John, Hudson's Hope, Mile Wonowon, Whitehorse and Tatshenshini-Alsek Provincial Park, where I've paused and looked around. The last named is a truly wild place in the extreme northwestern corner of this province where Alaska, British Columbia, Yukon, and many tall mountains and massive amounts of snow, rock and shifting ice come together. There are a few places on the far side of the Rocky Mountains in Alberta—Jasper, Banff, Red Deer, Rocky Mountain House, Fort Macleod and Waterton—where I've lingered for a few days, and others, like Writing-on-Stone out on the open prairies down south, that I've seen but hardly know at all.

Two of the various occupations I've worked at, as a parole officer in 1972, and for the Union of BC Indian Chiefs in 1973, both out of Prince George, necessitated that I travel; thus, I have stopped to do business of one kind or another at a large majority of the inhabited Indian Reserves in the BC Interior. Over the years, then and since, I have gained a general sense of the lay of the land and run of the rivers across much of this western land we are so privileged to inhabit and admire.

I like to see the country, and so does my partner, Marne; we enjoy travelling together and have done so for years. Recently, in the continued spirit of visiting and revisiting interesting places out here in the West, Marne and I decided we would drive north to Jasper, then veer slowly south along the Icefields Parkway in the shadow of the great Rocky Mountain chain through Banff and Kananaskis to Longview on Highway 22. Marne had not done that awe-inspiring drive before, and I wanted to share the experience with her. From some point south of Longview we would cut across the foothills and ranchlands of southern Alberta to Writing-on-Stone Park on the Milk River north of the American border. We chose to travel in late August–early September to avoid traffic and bugs if possible; our intention was to go at a relaxed pace, overnighting in motels or campsites according to the weather and whatever showed up.

Of course we would stop first at Darfield, north of Barriere on the North Thompson River, where I had lived for four impressionable young years after the war, and where my old schoolmate Kenny Schilling and his wife, Joy, live now. We looked forward to doing some exploring in Wells Grey Park, too. The weather was damp, the country sublime, and it was a pleasure to see our good friends again. We slowed up at Rearguard Falls on the upper Fraser River where Marne spotted large salmon, most likely springs (chinooks), resting in pools partway up the rapids. Those fish, having swum close to five hundred tough miles upstream from tidewater, are true miracles, and we stopped in reverence to watch them. We were impressed as well, a little farther up the highway, by the fleeting sight of massive, stone-faced Mount Robson in partial clouds and rain, a wall of rock and frozen snow, brooding. Is it possible that a mountain can maintain a sullen mood over millennia? I guess to a mountain, even a young peak in the Rocky Mountain range, itself a recent wrinkle in the tectonic scheme of things and part of "the marrow of the continent" (as the old-time mountain men used to say), a thousand years is as nothing.

Is it possible that a mountain can maintain a sullen mood over millennia?

We camped for several nights outside Jasper and observed some of the rich animal life in the area, highlights being a lone bighorn ram poised on a rock point, a silhouette above us; a large herd of ewes and lambs resting and chewing at roadside; and a small, traffic-halting elk herd dominated by a statuesque, nonchalant bull and a bossy lead cow. Back at camp, we were visited each evening by an unduly tame, slate-coloured junco, taking timeouts from food-bit gathering to fluff up its feathers and warm itself by our fire as we sat there. On our last night near Jasper we experienced our first serious rainfall, causing us to hit the road early the next morning.

As we travelled down along the big mountains, we'd tarry a while at certain places for walks and good views, or to investigate some of the haunts of our culture hero David Thompson, the great explorer and mapmaker. We drove and hiked through the upper watersheds of the North Saskatchewan and Athabasca Rivers to get a sense of their headwaters and the approaches to Howse and Athabasca Passes across the spine of the Rockies. Thompson found safe routes through both passes in the years 1807 and 1811 respectively. His objective was to establish fur trading networks and posts on the far side of the western mountains in the Kootenay and Columbia River Valleys, always with an eye to eventually reaching the Pacific Ocean. He finally did so via the lower Columbia in the summer of 1811, reading the stars and charting his route with characteristic patience and precision all along the way.

Marne and I drove the Thompson Highway to the national historic site and museum at Rocky Mountain House, out east on the plains. The North West Company fur fort there on the North Saskatchewan River served as Thompson's home base and supply post for his explorations. It was a thrill to parallel his path along the open, rolling Kootenay Plains (now partially flooded by man-made Abraham Lake) on a sunny late afternoon. Poplars were turning their autumn yellow already; the lake and sky were a bright, bright blue and the mountains were shining. But at our campsite at Bighorn River the following morning early, we were not even slightly thrilled to be rained out once again. This time, a hard rain fell long enough to seep through the corners of my thoroughly used, old tent. As we mopped up and packed, I began to wonder if these damp, dawn wake-ups and quick getaways might just wear us down.

Due to bursitis, a mild arthritic condition that I've managed carefully for years, my hips ache at night from the pressure of my bodyweight on them. I tend especially to lose deep sleep when I'm on hard ground in strange places, and my ability to get proper rest, night after night, becomes much reduced. I was getting edgy, I regret to say—enough to try even Marne's patience. Old age creeps in on heavy feet, creaky joints and a tired mind.

After a long and increasingly sunny drive down the Bow and Highwood Valleys via Banff and Kananaskis, punctuated by a short stop and gaze beside moving, sun-bright, mountain waters near the divide, we reached Longview in the late afternoon. We rented a room at the motel, which happens to be across from the Longview Community Hall. I recalled that Canadian song-writing and singing hero Ian Tyson had recorded at least one of his fine CDs in that very hall. Just down the street, near the Longview beef-jerky store and production plant, there is an attractive coffee shop-cum-Western whatnot shop called the Navaho Mug, clearly inspired by Tyson's spirit and presence; "Navaho Rug," co-written with Tom Russell, is one of his best-known songs. This open rolling foothills country has been Tyson's home for many years now, and most of his finely crafted, authentically detailed songs are firmly grounded right here and throughout rural southern Alberta. His horse-ranch home is somewhere not far away; local folks do not and will not let on where.

Marne and I went for a wonderfully pleasant walk in the dusky evening with the last sunlight slanting in from behind the peaks in the west; the hay fields, poplar groves and range all in soft shades of late-evening purples; and the feel of high prairie air cooling, as we strolled. Next morning we drove south down the scenic "Cowboy Trail" (Highway 22), east of the Livingstone Range, to the Crowsnest Highway. This is the general neighbourhood of ex-park ranger Sid Marty, another of my land-based literary exemplars and author of some very good books on this territory: *Men for the Mountains* and *Headwaters* are two that stand out for me. We turned left at Lundbreck and headed east and southeast for Writing-on-Stone Provincial Park, off Highway 4 a few miles past the village of Milk River.

All along we'd had the quiet sense that Writing-on-Stone was our conclusive destination, the underlying reason we were travelling these roads. We had paid a quick visit there on a trip to Maple Creek, the Cypress Hills and Grasslands National Park in southern Saskatchewan several summers earlier, but our stay was cut short by a light, early September snowstorm. We began a walk through the hoodoos and a few of the closest rock writings but a chill wind and driven snow numbing our faces and hands soon put a stop to that. Our connection with Writing-on-Stone was hardly started and we knew it.

As we veered southeast towards the Milk River turnoff, the three conical buttes that comprise the Sweetgrass Hills (Ka'toyissiksi) rose up above the horizon in front of us like living, moving beings. For anyone headed through this open country to Writing-on-Stone (A'i'si'nai'pi) in the old pre-settler, horse days, those peaks, clear or blue in the distance, served as a hard-to-miss directional guide (unless socked in by snow, rain or dust storms). I have

The Sweetgrass Hills, as seen looking south from Writing-on-Stone Park on the Milk River. Photo courtesy of Marne St. Claire.

a feeling that those two outstanding landforms—the cluster of dark hills just across the US border pointing to the sky world, and the chain of extended coulees cut into the ground—were perceived traditionally as facets of the same underlying energy.

Writing-on-Stone Park is a stunningly beautiful place: an oasis of cottonwood trees, willows, rich bird and animal life, with the moving waters of Milk River running through it all. The Milk River, the fundamental reason for the significance and even the basic existence of the place, rises in the mountains of northwest Montana. It flows, or rather meanders, to the northeast, shifting gradually east, then southeast, till it crosses the US border again and joins the great Missouri River southeast of the Cypress Hills. It is not a large river; its volume is further reduced by irrigation, and it is certainly not fast-flowing. Its colour is milky from the mud it carries, and there are strong hints of rock-flour blue-green in it, a reminder that its source is high in the snow- and ice-bearing Rocky Mountains.

As slow as it is, the Milk River has eroded its way through soft, sedimentary sandstone so that now its flat alluvial valley lies some one to two hundred feet below the prairie mantle. Further erosion of the stratified rock by wind, rain, freezing and thawing, and flooding meltwaters has created a multitude of vertical pinnacles, hoodoos by the hundreds that stand like humans, singly or in groups, along the steep rock edges of the valley. Mountaineers, in such close connection to the mountains they climb, ascribe liveliness to similar rock formations in high places, referring to them as "gendarmes." So it is not hard to comprehend that indigenous folks saw hoodoos as lively beings; they have presence, especially in their sheer numbers and scale, and there are whole committees of them shifting position as the shadows change, standing there in their myriad variations to greet you silently, or maybe not so silently if a wind is blowing, as you pass by. Aboriginal people hold the Writing-in-Stone area in awe and to this day are cautious and mindful about venturing into it.

Writing-on-Stone may be life-supporting and attractive, but there are virtually no archaeological indications that pre-contact humans actually lived here. They certainly visited the place, carefully and with intention, for at least three thousand years and probably a lot longer. All along the river, mainly on sun- and south-facing sandstone walls, are petroglyphs, carvings incised in the rock, hundreds and hundreds of them, silent statements that this place was all Indian land not long ago, claimed by the Niitsi'tapi, Blackfoot people, most recently, and probably Shoshonean peoples from the south before them. No doubt hunting and raiding parties from other plains groups—Cree, Gros Ventre, Assiniboine, Crow and others—also passed through. The coming of the horse to the northwestern plains in the 1730s radically expanded the capacity of aboriginal peoples to range far and wide across the land.

For its many winding miles, the river's broad canyon is a water-worn slice out of the surface of the great mother earth. That long indentation in the ground makes the mud-blue river a potent, lively place, a holy place, a place indigenous, hunting people could not take lightly. Given the precariousness of their livelihood and the total focus required of them, primal hunters and gatherers saw and felt things in wild nature with a degree of subtlety and acuity far beyond the experience of members of modern-day urban cultures. Such an elongated, womb-like hole in the earth in a shamanistic world was perceived as an aperture to the underworld, a place of unimaginable power and danger that heroes and vision seekers ventured into at their risk.

Marne and I arrived at Writing-on-Stone in the late afternoon after the long-distance drive from Longview. The September shadows were lengthening but the place was still warm from the day's sun. We set up camp with the notion that we would take it easy now, turn in early and walk the Hoodoo Trail the next morning. The evening was pleasant; we were alone and unbothered, but as light changed to dark, the Milk River Valley became more obviously lively with the sounds of night creatures.

At nightfall, mule deer came out in numbers to feed; they seemed to me to be in a hurry. Some munched so close to the tent I could hear the breath expelling in tiny bursts from their nostrils and the sound of grass ripping as they tore off fast mouthfuls. Their hard little hoofs crunched on the gravelly ground. Occasionally one or another would call out with a sheep-like bleating sound, I presume to maintain contact with each other. I realized later that probably they were making nighttime hay, as it were, before the next storm hit.

Coyotes yipped and howled in the distance, carrying on for much of the night; mourning doves cooed, low-flying geese gabbled overhead, and three great horned owls began hooting back and forth, two nearby, the other some distance downriver. The call of one of the close ones had a cadence too rapid for the usual "who's awake, me too" call we are so used to hearing. This bird seemed unpractised in the fine art of mature, nighttime mating hoots; there were intimations of "who's awake…," but his notes were high-pitched and vague, and his call lacked authority, as if he was being pushed by nature to participate, ready or not.

Much later, in darkest night, we awoke to the sound of wind blowing hard through the cottonwood trees above us. It was not so loud at first, but it rapidly accelerated to an almighty roar; the sound came through in great waves

The Milk River flowing from west (right) to east to reach the Missouri River, eventually. Photo courtesy of Marne St. Claire.

as if the wind was breathing in big, gulping breaths. "Oceanic" was the word Marne used to describe it; "overwhelming" is a word I might choose. I would have expected the wind's force against our tent walls to be more violent, but its momentum took it mostly through treetops, I think because of the elevation of the open prairie above the valley bottom.

We lay there for a long time, kept wide awake by the power and frenzy above us. The air was electric, and some of that charge was coursing powerfully up and down my backbone, sharpening my body-mind attention and reminding me that I was part of something ineffable. About daybreak the wind began losing its intensity, quite quickly in fact; suddenly rain was coming down hard, and the ground outside was soon covered in sodden cottonwood leaves, small, broken-off branches, and standing water. Anything we'd hung up out there was over in faraway Manyberries (southeastern Alberta) by now. When it was light enough to see, I donned my rain gear, and while Marne stuffed our bags inside, I trotted back and forth in the pelting rain to the Pathfinder, performing our well-rehearsed fast-packing-getaway team routine. The tent we packed wet.

Even with practice, it takes a while to pack the vehicle in a semi-organized and secure fashion, and we noticed as we began driving away that the rain

Rock formations at Writing-on-Stone. Photo courtesy of Marne St. Claire.

seemed to be slackening. The sky was definitely lightening and brightening. So we decided we might as well do the hoodoo walk after all; it's what we had come here for. We knew the trip would have something of a holy quality to it, so we deliberately left our camera, binoculars and interpretive trail brochure back at the camp. We wished simply to walk through the place, experiencing it in slow depth if we could, without getting too heady and distracted. We did take a little tobacco with us to be sure we left something in acknowledgment.

The walk along the cliff bases was a relief and a quiet pleasure. The air and ground had been washed clean, and the grasses on the low flats, the shrubs and brush along the river—willows, river birch, chokecherry and saskatoons—all looked greener and brighter than they had the day before. The small birds in trees and shrubs or on open ground everywhere, golden-crowned kinglets, catbirds, various grassland sparrows, mourning doves, a few swooping swallows, were too preoccupied with feeding to hide. Towhees scratched loudly in the underbrush. In the soft morning light, the layered and capped sandstone hoodoos, pinnacles, arches, points, ledges, small caves and holes, a labyrinth of them, looked scrubbed. The terrain around us, honey-coloured, dull orange, reddish-ochre, dark, all shades of sandy stone, seemed engraved against the coulees and rolling grasslands on the other side of the river.

We made our way through and up and down and over and around the stone topography, a good clamber for us both. We stopped often to spot and admire the many incised, often simple, even crude, figures; some, in a poor light and eroded, were hard to discern. After a while we recognized that although the images may seem simple, they are subtly stylized and abbreviated, probably a kind of pictorial writing meant to be read and understood. Most images depict identifiable subjects: various wild animals, ungulates and grizzly bears mostly; tipis; travois; men standing; men on horses, natives and a few non-natives both; horses and more horses, herds of them, even wagons; warriors in battle, arrows or long guns pointed at each other; weapons, including spears, swords, bows and arrows, rifles, bullets in mid-trajectory; some men with large decorated shields—all carefully, even artfully, rendered. Many images are eroding rapidly. There are weathered streaks of red ochre paint and occasional red-painted or charcoaled figures and markings here and there throughout. One dark circular ochre figure on a high rock face above the valley looks sharp-edged and recent.

From the writings of several anthropologists and archaeologists, I learned that there were several phases to the evolution of these images in stone over time, ranging from pre-horse and pre-contact to detailed horse-dominated and historic periods. Some writers state that, paralleling the arrival of the horse and the rifled gun, these shifts in content and style suggest a change of emphasis from such collective activities as buffalo jumps to more individual accomplishments, like "counting coup" and horse stealing. Some of the panels depict historic events, accurate even to the precise numbers of warriors and tipis present, as in the detailed "great battle scene" circa 1866. Many images are of a strongly supernatural nature.

Probably the core fact of Writing-on-Stone is that young men and shamans came to these places to deprive themselves of food, water, sleep, warmth and human company in search of visions, spirit-visitations that might help them comprehend their life path and gain power and authority in this unfathomable, and frequently dangerous, competitive world. Often the outcomes of those lonely, lengthy, spiritual vigils spent fasting, praying, chanting, meditating, dreaming would be transcribed in careful detail on stone panels along the sandstone cliffs near their vision sites. Those incised images are archetypically shamanistic: some human figures are transparent and skeletal, indicating transformations unfolding; some beings are part human–part animal, or spirit-beings in human form in various degrees of metamorphosis; some stand with their arms upraised and long fingers splayed, demonstrating a shaman's awe in the face of the mighty forces he is contending with.

The Writing-on-Stone vision-seeking sites up and down the Milk River are not typical, though the place is self-evidently an entity of considerable power. Most of the many questing sites in the region are located in high and lonely places, like the Porcupine and Sweetgrass Hills, where they command direct views of certain outstanding mountains nearby. Such high peaks, including, most notably, imposing Chief Mountain to the southeast of Waterton National Park, are perceived as "charged with spiritual energy," as research scientist John Dormaar puts it. Vision-seeking sites are often marked by piles, or "nests," of local rock, stacked sometimes in a U shape to provide some limited protection for the seeker. There is not the same need for such nests at Writing-on-Stone, and I believe it is significant, given that the site is not high and lonely, that the Sweetgrass Hills to the south are visible from up on the open shortgrass prairie and along the tops of the cliffs above the valley bottom. Writing-on-Stone, as beautiful and powerful as it is, would not be as powerful a place, I think, without the balancing male presence of and connection to the Sweetgrass Hills.

In rock writings along the Milk River and elsewhere, to paint on or cut into the sandstone to create images is to maintain their liveliness; this merges the energy of the rock itself with the original vision events and the pictured forms. In a myth-time world beyond time, all entities are related. Even the bedrock is seen to be permeable.

Rock carving of a horse, one of many horses depicted at Writing-on-Stone. Photo courtesy of Marne St. Claire.

Back at the campsite in the early afternoon, we spread the tent out to dry and set it up again, then ate a slow picnic lunch. Marne thought she'd walk up to the visitor centre and look through the little museum there; I was suffering the effects of foreshortened nights, especially the most recent one, and felt exhausted and stupid. I wanted to catch up on my lost sleep if I could, so I stretched out for a while. After staring at the top of the tent for an hour or two, I decided to join Marne.

As I walked up the path to the centre, I realized I was not functioning well; my balance was poor and I barely knew where I was. I walked hesitantly into the museum, muttered a weak "Hi" to Marne and tried to make sense of some of the presentations. I recognized some titles and place names and knew in a vague way what most of the main words meant, but I simply could not understand what the shows were about. I knew I'd be better to just sit down and rest; I told Marne that I needed to still my being for a while, and spent the next three-quarters of an hour looking out and down at the flowing

Rock-capped hoodoos in late afternoon at Writing-on-Stone. Photo courtesy of Marne St. Claire.

blue-green river and alluvial valley, the rolling plains and hills in the far distance, watching and absorbing the sun's light and warmth coming through the tall windows. My mind was mostly blank. At closing time we left.

By this time Marne was becoming thoroughly worried, especially as I could barely navigate my way down the steep path to valley bottom level; normally I'm fairly nimble. I was aware that I was incoherent in thought and word, and the helplessness of it frightened me. We found ourselves at the start of the trail to the hoodoos and rock pictures, and instinctively, no words spoken, we began slowly to walk along it.

The late-afternoon September sun was lowering; colours were rich, the air warm but cooling, the sky bluer than blue, and the entire valley, but particularly the hoodoos and rock formations in front of me, seemed lit up by golden light. I found myself substantially overwhelmed by everything I saw.

I began exclaiming out loud and often, using the same few words each time. "That's amazing," I would say as I turned to look at a new rock formation suffused in sunlight and its own rich colours, shades, surfaces, shapes, textures. Marne counted "That's amazing" thirteen times, and now she was really concerned. It was not so much the sandstone, but the colours themselves I was looking into and exclaiming at; I could see what pale orange or sand-hued or red ochre truly were, because I could see right into them, or so I thought. After a while we sat and watched the evening subside to darker dusky tones, the shades of nighttime coming slowly down around us. Marne talked to a man from Edmonton for a bit, and I sat mainly silent, content to be a part of the landscape. Then we walked slowly back to our campsite for an easy supper, something simple, least effort, and a cool drink of water from the camp pump in the last of the light.

Marne is the queen of loving support at all times, and that evening in discussion we came to the conclusion that in my significantly sleep-deprived state, parts of my persona, my ego, the face I normally present to the world, had become very tired and fallen away for a while. Inadvertently, my fatigue had triggered a mildly altered way of seeing, something thinly equivalent to a shamanistic vision, a partial, parallel version of what might have been sought and experienced by seekers in earlier times here in these rock-writing sites in a land of hunting and warring, vision questing and moving from place to place.

People have gone in search of guidance, power and reassurance for millennia; over all that time, men (and women) have seriously deprived and surrendered themselves for visions in places of power and permeability, places like Writing-on-Stone. This magnificent valley is suffused, not just with light and the presence of ten thousand rock formations, a rich range of wildlife and a beautiful blue-green river running through it, but with the collective consciousness of centuries of prayerful acknowledgment and practice.

There is no reason to believe we are not affected by the qualities of places, whether we note it or not, especially places like Writing-on-Stone. If this is not a setting of power and depth, then I don't know one. This is the site, after all, of the largest collection of aboriginal rock writing in Canada, in a location that has been known to be holy since before history, since the last ice, since myth time, "since time immemorial" as aboriginal elders still say. To be in this place is inevitably to be touched by it.

Across the river, some distance back from the water's edge and opening from the south is Police Coulee. Near its mouth, on a large flat, stands a replica of the North West Mounted Police post à la 1897. It was a border post for some thirty years before and after the turn of the twentieth century. Around and under where the building stands are the midden remnants of an ancient camping place for prehistoric aboriginal visitors passing through. For ten thousand years, at least, aboriginal peoples have followed the stars, the watercourses and the buffalo back and forth across this open country on foot and, for some decades, by horse. The Milk River is fordable here, and ancient trails crossed each other at this point.

> *To be in this place is inevitably to be touched by it.*

Writing-on-Stone has become a crossroads of a different sort. Now, we newcomers arrive from all directions in our automobiles to camp here under the cottonwoods, enjoy this lovely river valley, walk the trail of hoodoos and shake our heads in varying degrees of wonder at the mysteries of the rock-writing panels. We come to this place to be here, to attempt to see it for what it is and was, and perhaps gain a little understanding of the people who carved those images over all those centuries. We may ask why those first people are mostly gone from around here now and how we visitors came to be here in our numbers in their place. Some will be curious about the first peoples' ways of living in this world of rolling grasslands, running rivers, long winters and big sky. Do the old first folks' ways of seeing and being in this harsh, beautiful, vast land overlap in any basic manner with our view of it all in these fast times? Do our paths cross? Can we know this is a living, transformative world in which we live and breathe? Can we say honestly yet that we belong here? How have your dreams, visions and grace moments been informing you?

These varied western lands are a true wonder, no matter which side of the shining mountains you happen to be walking.

AROUND BIG BAR MOUNTAIN

Within and around the earth,
within and around the hills,
within and around the mountain,
your authority returns to you.

—Tewa Prayer

MANY A NINETEENTH-CENTURY GOLD SEEKER IN THE MAD RUSH TO HOPED-FOR
riches in the British Columbia Interior found moiling for gold a tedious and
typically fruitless task, short on easy access to the motherlode. Having passed
through some of the finest and most attractive land imaginable on their way
north to the Cariboo goldfields, many of those seekers eventually discovered
more effective and lasting ways to make a living from the country. Herbert
Bowe, Raphael Valenzuela, Isadore Gaspard (Conte de Verespeuch), William
Laing Meason, Moses (Moise) Pigeon, John Koster, Joseph Haller, Conrad
Kostering, Phil Grinder, William Wycott and others, were quick to re-think
and settle on good land in choice, accessible locations, chiefly on lower, open
benches and creek drainages along the Fraser River. Their intent was to raise
horses and cattle, and perhaps grow farm produce to sell to would-be miners passing by. With his partner Samuel Leander "Charlie" Brown, Isadore
Gaspard introduced the growing and milling of wheat to the Dog Creek
area in 1862. Their grist mill was the first on the BC mainland. Others like

Valenzuela, Grinder and Wycott were or had been packers or teamsters and sought low-elevation pastures with light snowfall where they could winter their work animals.

Not only did many early immigrants stay to make a living in the region, but some, including all the pioneer men listed above, had aboriginal wives with whom they raised families. Some of their daughters became ranchers' wives, mothers of ranch children, and the ancestors of future owners of some of the historic Interior ranches we know and admire today.

These men and their new-world families accomplished more than the fundamental, and sometimes all-consuming, task of survival. I believe many came to feel that they had found their place in this world. The settled-in aspects of older ranch headquarters in their invariably attractive and well-watered settings—places like Dog Creek, the O K Ranch, the B.C. Cattle Company at Canoe Creek, Alkali Lake, Deer Park, Riske Creek Ranch, Chilco Ranch, Empire Valley, the original (and present) Gang Ranch sites, to list some prime examples from the Cariboo-Chilcotin region—speak to this possibility. The fact that, generations later, descendants of many of those first homesteaders still live in the region affirms this also.

Some other individuals and families who came later to settle in more marginal locations and times may not have been so fortunate, nor so persevering or long-lasting. Many of those folks have passed on through: who knows where they and their descendents have dispersed to? Above all, of course, aboriginal peoples lived, survived and thrived on this land since the retreat of the glaciers eleven thousand years ago, "since time immemorial" as they say. It is intriguing to consider that descendents of those first peoples, in small numbers most likely, may have been among the first owners and keepers of cattle in the Interior of this province.

Now I find myself rattling about the open grassland slopes of Big Bar Mountain in the gloaming, that period of evening half-light and stillness before dark descends. I am with rancher Lawrence Joiner, whom I have only just met, in his well-worn pickup. The third member of the trio is his collie dog, an intelligent personage named Zipper, who at this moment is seated firmly in his rightful place, upright on the front seat, smelling new smells, checking things out, running inventory, making sure all is as it should be and leaning into me hard, mostly for the warmth I think, but also perhaps to remind me that I am impinging slightly on that selfsame rightful place of his. Overall, I'd say Zipper is quite forbearing about the whole situation. His partner and boss, Mr. Joiner, owns this outfit: these slopes we are pounding about on, the summer and winter ranges all around, most of the hayfields down

Now I find myself rattling about the open grassland slopes of Big Bar Mountain in the gloaming, that period of evening half-light and stillness before dark descends.

along the Fraser River benches, the old O K Ranch headquarters on Big Bar Creek: all the many, varied parts that make up this operation.

"Let's go," Lawrence had said earlier, "I'll show you some places before it gets dark." So we jumped in the truck, Zipper assumed his place and off we went. Joiner has more work to squeeze in before nightfall. We are combining jobs, "multi-tasking" as they say in the urban world these days, hardly a new concept for a rancher. Lawrence is enthusiastic to show me some of the signs of local homesteading history, but it is springtime and his calving cows can't wait. There are newborn calves to find, check out and count, and a busted fence to repair. In between calf-spotting, we find clues to old-time settlers' homesites across the slopes, bits and pieces of detritus scattered here and there over the mountain, especially along this wide, mid-elevation, southwest-facing slope looking out over the Fraser River that we're on right now. I am practised in the fine art of finding hints of old places and old lives, but I would have missed much of what my guide is showing me now in this impending gloom. These are mostly the kinds of clues you either stumble upon or know. Lawrence Joiner knows his territory well.

Lawrence has carefully isolated his pregnant cows so he can keep track of them and their little brand-spanking-fresh, spindly legged, whiter-than-white-faced offspring, tottering or gamboling about. Unfortunately, some of the mums-to-be had decided, a day or two earlier, that they needed to

The O K Ranch headquarters on Big Bar Creek, originally the Joseph Haller Ranch, and currently owned and operated by Lawrence Joiner. Photo courtesy of Chris Schreiber.

be somewhere else and had leaned on the old wire fence till it fell over. I find myself helping dig post holes, me windily loosening soil, old post bits and rocks with a too-heavy crowbar, while he shovels. This was the kind of heavy labour I did forty or fifty years ago in my young logging years, but not recently. I wheeze, while Lawrence, who is older than I, casually and comfortably works on without obvious trace of effort. I say, demonstrating my mastery of understatement, "I seem to be getting out of shape." He says, with a degree of kindness, "It's all in what you're used to, I guess." We get some holes dug, ready for posts in the morning, and all the time I'm asking questions and he's responding with the basic facts of this darkening place and some of the people who used to live around here.

Finally Lawrence announces that it's getting too dark to work. We three climb in the truck and off we go again. He is rattling off names and details: who lived where, who's connected to who, who did what when, whose descendants still live around here, all of it happening so fast my tired brain is shifting on its axis. We are banging across the landscape, almost as much up and down as forward, so that even if I'd had my pen and notebook in hand, note-taking would have been pointless. I hang on and peer out and help my new doggy buddy maintain his position of staunch vigilance, trying the while to remember what I can. It has been a long and lively day for me already, but I am enthralled in a bone-weary, sore-eyed sort of way.

Lawrence is locating remnants of houses and barns: squared-off foundation mounds, dirt and stone, the occasional rectangular depression in the ground, the odd cabin site, rock root cellars, privy holes, a section of roadwork, old and now fenceless fence lines, plough furrows in the earth, hints of ditching and, up the hill near standing timber, the shadowy half-collapsed house lived in at one time by Miles Clink and his wife, Emily. Farther back, barely visible against a bank of dark fir trees, stands a roofless log barn, built, says Lawrence, by Billy Grinder, father to Henry Grinder, who himself took over the homestead, dry farmed it and, with his wife, Annie, raised a large family there. Annie's parents were Harry Higgenbottom and Mariah Wycott, daughter of the legendary William "Stranger" Wycott from above Wycott Flats up Churn Creek. In later years Henry worked for Harry Marriott at the O K Ranch and for the Gang Ranch, and developed a near-legendary reputation of his own as a great cowboy. Henry Grinder was still saddling up at age ninety the year he died.

His father, Billy, was an older son and heir to the original, the redoubtable Phil Grinder himself, who came into this country with the rest of the gold seekers in the 1860s rush. Now there are Grinder descendants all over the Cariboo country, some so embedded they are not even in the telephone book. I saw a winter-worn hunting camp a few years ago, over by Castellain Springs above the lower Chilcotin River, where a length of heavy, weathered, builder's paper hung from two trees with the name "GRINDER" written across it in large, red, surprisingly artful letters; obviously this was a sign left by hunters announcing it was Grinder-style "Party Time." Lawrence tells me that one of his long-time cowboys was Albert Grinder, younger brother to Henry and another Grinder of high repute. There are Grinders living around the Clinton area today who would have gotten their start, their leap into this world, their launch into relativity, at the modest homestead sites I am squinting at in the near-dark right now. Children played and laughed and cried, and their mothers worried about them, where these overgrown house shells still stand.

The first folks who came in numbers to settle up here on Big Bar Mountain appeared before the First World War. Homesteaders, some veterans of the war, continued to arrive through the '20s and into the '30s. These were people enticed by available land, desperation and the dubious prospect of dry farming. The theory (more like a hoax) was that if the hopeful farmer ploughed and broke the ground, the freshly opened earth, being dark, would attract rain, and the crop would get the moisture necessary to grow to maturity as promised. In other words, there would be no need to irrigate. In his book *Bad Land*, Jonathan Raban examines this massive land sales con-job, and the consequent dust storms and heartbreak, as it occurred on the dry plains of eastern Montana. The theory is called "dry farming," and it lured would-be farmers out to the great plains of North America by the thousands. Much of that dry plains country—the Palliser triangle in southwest Saskatchewan and southeast Alberta, and eastern Montana south of the border—was suitable, at best, for grazing stock, not sod-busting. Simply stated, there was not enough dependable rainfall.

There were small-scale equivalent "dry farms" around the Cariboo–Chilcotin in the BC Interior as well. Local examples include a small section of Empire Valley Ranch above the irrigated fields along Koster and Grinder Creeks, and some benchland west of the lower Chilcotin River in Gang Ranch territory, known to this day as the Dry Farm.

As Harry Marriott recounts in a chapter of his classic book *Cariboo Cowboy*, dry weather in the 1930s, and the usual array of homesteader hardships, drove these Big Bar Mountain people out, farmer by farmer, family by family. Those hapless, hard-working folks must have gotten sore necks peering into the sky in their search for rain clouds; they apparently got sufficient moisture for their crops about one year in five. Now, except for a single cow camp cabin by a usually flowing spring, there are no habitable buildings on the mountain. The last person to try to farm on Big Bar Mountain was Ronnie Marriott, son of Harry, in the late '40s, early '50s.

Harry Marriott would not have minded the farmers' demise too much, I think. In his interviews in *Tales of the Ranches*, part of the People in Landscape oral history series from the BC Archives, he admitted to having "something of what you might call a Cecil Rhodes complex," that is to say a strong "empire-building" urge for himself and his family. He said most ranchers of his time had that same competitive inclination, and from his perspective as a retired ranchman in 1964 he referred to it quite emphatically (and, I suspect, a touch ruefully) as "a disease." So for Marriott, with the backing of Vancouver financier George Harrison, the plight of the Big Bar Mountain settlers presented a series of opportunities for him to buy them out and expand his growing O K Ranch, headquartered up Big Bar Creek. And now Lawrence Joiner is the owner of the outfit some seventy-plus years later.

Henry Grinder, Big Bar Mountain farmer and cowboy of long standing. Henry was a grandson of Phil and Nancy (Kala'llst) Grinder, original settlers in the area. Photo courtesy of Don Logan.

I mention Harry Marriott and his book to Lawrence, and he responds, with a knowing look, that when he read *Cariboo Cowboy* he noticed that Marriott did not mention certain local characters at all. He pauses, "Like Riley." That would be James Riley, whose range included an area up Big Bar Creek, now a small Forest Service campsite and fishing pond known as Riley's Dam. Riley once owned the old, original Joe Haller ranch that later became the nucleus for Marriott's O K Ranch, across from where the Big Bar Guest Ranch is now.

"Oh?" I ask hopefully, and Lawrence proceeds to recount some long-standing historic events that might in some circles be called gossip, sufficiently personal, given possible living descendants around, that discretion prevents me from repeating. It has occurred to me that much of what we refer to as regional or local history might well be called "high-level gossip." It's the personal detail that can make local history so lively.

Dark has fully descended, and Lawrence announces his frustration that we can no longer see anything much unless it is square in our headlights. He had wanted to show me the Wilkinson place and the rodeo grounds down below the road by a grove of firs at a place called Rodeo Flats, as well as the old Cariboo prospector's trail up from Big Bar lower down in the trees, and the cabin where Harry Marriott lived when he was minding cattle for the Gang Ranch on the Crows Bar winter range. That was before he started his own outfit.

I'm surprised that line cabin is so close and still partially standing, and say so; then I ask how far off the track it was. It's about a mile, he tells me, and I file that information away for future reference. I had thought the cabin to be much closer to Crows Bar Creek. The Henry Koster family, whose descendents are the current owners of B.C. Cattle Company at Canoe Creek, lived and ranched at Crows Bar in their early days. In the late 1920s, the Kosters bought Empire Valley Ranch and owned and ran it as part of their overall operation for three decades before selling it. Jack Koster, oldest son of Henry Senior, ran the Canoe Creek outfit for years. He died just recently, leaving son Warren and wife Selina in charge. Jack Koster was reputed to be as tough as he always was right up to his last days.

I'm curious about the mad cow issue and its restrictions on our beef exports to the US, so I ask Lawrence how much it has affected him. He says it would set him back quite seriously and that he'd need to log some timber to try to make up the difference. I ask where, and Lawrence tells me that there's good, old-growth fir up the hill right in behind the old Grinder place that looks easy enough to get at. He points at some big dark trees on the ridge above us, barely visible against the starry night sky.

Having worked at logging in my young years, my first response is to visualize the mess yarding, loading and hauling logs close in behind the old homesteads might make. Then, as I consider the larger picture, I recall the rapidity of regeneration in this country, especially on a sunny, southern exposure;

poplars, lodgepole pine and willows, grasses, road weeds and brush will grow back quickly. In time, the scent of wild roses will fill the June air and the pure red bracts of Indian paintbrush will brighten up the undergrowth as before. The road will become just another grown-in track, mud in spring, dust in summer: ruts, potholes and washouts, dandelions, mullein and pearly everlasting, and knapweed, unfortunately, along the margins. We can so surely depend on the relentless force and logical unfolding of wild nature.

The continuingly good-hearted Lawrence announces that I might as well park my rig in the yard at his place; he has some interesting old pictures that he thinks I should see. We bang our way down off the mountain, me bouncing in and out, opening and closing gates, disturbing the sleepy, but polite, Zipper, and find ourselves quickly at the O K Ranch yard. We pick up my Pathfinder at the bottom of the hill, and I look for a level place to park in preparation for a comfortable sleep in it overnight, before joining Lawrence in his small and somewhat dusty kitchen. He hauls out a big, old-fashioned, pre-emptor series lands map and a large aerial photo to show me the extent of his hold-ings, and a little stack of small browned photographs he found in the house somewhere. The pictures are very interesting: mostly a series of slightly faded snaps of men riding, or attempting to ride, bucking horses at what looks like a primitive rodeo, presumably at Rodeo Flats, and people lined up, watching. The riders are all in various stages of quick, unwilling separation from their mounts; one man departing his horse is in mid-air, stretched out straight as an ironing board at a 45-degree angle to the saddle, boots pointed at the sky. He looks like he's been shot from a cannon. That lad is about to gain a bit more elevation, turn a tight, gravity-bound arc, and drop south in a hurry. The way he's aimed, if he's agile, he should just about land on his feet.

There are several especially intriguing aspects to these pictures: first, the good numbers of men, women and children there are, gathered, stand-ing, watching and, I'm sure, happily socializing, all dressed up in their finest. Rodeo Flats would have been centrally located for the farmers up on the mountain and below, down Big Bar Creek. Lawrence states there were homesteads scattered all over and three schools. I interpret the latter

Harry Marriott, founder of the O K Ranch and author of *Cariboo Cowboy*, circa 1935. Photo courtesy of Don Logan.

reference to mean that the school was housed in three different locations over the years; one site he is sure of was by Poison Lake on the way in; another, I learn later, was situated at the Wilkinson place (lot 4212). Until fairly recently, the Howling Dog Community Hall and social hub had stood sturdy but unused these latter years, not a great distance below the brow of the hill down along the creek.

Some of the men appear to be dressed in clean, white shirts. It occurs to me that those shirts would, of course, have been hand-washed in hard water. Those washer-wives would have had hands like claws if my mother's reddened and knuckled hands after five years of such hard labour, in my young Interior childhood, were any indication. Mum never complained. Nor did she protest life later in a large but isolated logging camp on the north end of Vancouver Island after we left Darfield, up the North Thompson, in 1950. At least our new up-coast home, Port McNeill, had diesel-generators to power, however intermittently, such wondrously modern conveniences as washing machines, clothes wringers, refrigerators and light bulbs.

Affixed to the top rodeo picture is a tag with the names "Stobie" and "Phillipine" in very neat writing, and the date "1932." This intrigues me. What would those references mean? The former would have to refer to Andy Stobie, or an offspring. Stobie was the Scottish manager of the Gang Ranch after the turn of the twentieth century, and something of an institution. He was the man who befriended and hired young Harry Marriott in 1912. There is a lake named after him up Little Gaspard Creek in the backcountry behind the Gang. (I saw a big, dark, high-humped grizzly crossing the road near there just three days later.)

The latter name refers to Simon Phillipine, who lived down by Lone Cabin Creek south of Empire Valley Ranch on the west side of the Fraser River, and who pre-empted property there in 1943. Apparently he was related to James Riley's wife, who was a Pigeon. Phillipine would have been among the last of the old-time settlers in that remote country, after the Chinese gold miners, Magee the packer after whom McGhee Flats are named, the Higgenbottom family and the sheepherders. He died in 1948. I walked that long walk down there one glorious, bird-lively spring day a few years ago. There were still signs of Phillipine's old buildings, a cabin at Hog Lake and a pair of log houses above a small hayfield on a precarious, north-facing bench on the south side of the Lone Cabin Creek gorge. The trail into and through that place would spook a goat. He irrigated, out of Simon's Creek it looks like, but the unaccustomed weight of water on that steep, overhanging, clay hillside caused much of his hayfield to slump off into the canyon. On an even narrower bench just west, a small round corral stood; obviously he trained horses, but then so did everybody. I read somewhere that he "died in his cabin with his boots on," and that his horses and their descendants ran wild for years after in that lonely country south of his place. I'm guessing that Pony Valley in the hills off French Bar Creek was named after Phillipine's gone-wild horses.

So who in 1932 would have taken those pictures? That year "1932" is congruent, given the people's clothing styles and the fact that, in the early '30s, the Big Bar Mountain area still had a sizable population. At first I'd wondered if that careful printer was Mr. Marriott himself, and if it was he or perhaps his wife, Peg, who took the photos. However, I learned a while back that it was John Hogarth, the teacher at Jesmond School at the time, who was the photographer. Incidentally, Peggy Marriott lived to a great age and died in Kamloops very recently.

And why is Andy Stobie's name associated here? Certainly he was long dead by 1932, though he has descendants around Cache Creek, so I've heard. There is a last picture in the collection, a different size and shape and more

Bronc riding at Rodeo Flats, Big Bar Mountain, circa 1932. Photo courtesy of Don Logan.

aged and faded, of various people, several looking partly native, by a stark but substantial ranch building on a bare sagebrush slope. The fine detail of the photo is excellent. The folks appear to be in late-nineteenth-century apparel, and there are various vintage artifacts around. A lone rider on a skinny horse passes casually across the sagebrush hillside up behind the house, stopping his horse long enough to pose for the photographer. Stobie would surely have been around this part of the country sufficiently early to know this ranch and most of the people in that fabulous old picture.

The notation on the back of the photo states this was the Kostering Ranch house at Null Springs, down on the Fraser River east of the mouth of Big Bar Creek. It was originally pre-empted by Joseph Null in 1873 and bought by Conrad Kostering later on. One of the hills south of Big Bar Creek is called Mount Kostering, and there is a Kostering Creek not far away. The Kostering Ranch was known locally as the Sheep and Wool Place; it and the benchland

and hayfields around it are owned now by Lawrence Joiner. He mentions he was just down there earlier in the day, irrigating. I had driven by it on my way upriver from High Bar and noticed the tall shade trees that marked its location across the fields below the road. The shed on the left in the old picture still stands. I expect the ranch had been a staging location in the days when the sheep herds driven over from around Kamloops were ferried over the Fraser at Big Bar, a laborious process, to summer graze in the mountains west of the river.

The trail into and through that place would spook a goat.

My eyes feel as if they are about to fall out of my head, and it is definitely time to hit the sack. Lawrence agrees as he has to be up and out of here at first light himself; he has that fence to finish and more calves to check. Maybe I should have offered to stay and help, especially given Lawrence's quick, generous offer to show me around, in spite of my unasked-for intrusion into his life, but at the moment all I can think of is what a wonderful place the inside of my new "three-season" sleeping bag will be. It's been an inspirational day.

I had gotten a nice, early start from the Lower Mainland that morning, and the miles had passed by quickly. I gassed and watered up at Clinton, and turned down the cutoff road to Kelly Lake and the Jesmond road north. The weather was clear and cool. It was so bright and shiny, in fact, and the hour early enough that when I came to the turnoff to Cougar Point, I thought I would take that sheer, switchbacked road down to High Bar on the Fraser River. I wanted to get a sense of the wild liveliness of those low-elevation sagebrush benches in the freshness of springtime, and I knew I'd probably spot some spring birds winging north. As well, I hankered for a peek at lonely Watson Bar and the several forgotten little ranches over there across the river on the west (Chilcotin) side. I had the vague notion I might find a level spot somewhere on Big Bar Mountain later, preferably with a good early-morning view, where I could park my Pathfinder for the night.

This was the same steep road that, years back when Marne and I had driven to the turnout at the top of the hill, curved abruptly out of sight down into that hazy, bleached Fraser River light. The big river ran south somewhere at the bottom of it. The sign at the top said "23% grade, drive with extreme caution" or "Go at your peril" or words to that effect. My almost infallibly charming partner read it and said, firmly, "No, not me. You can drive down there if you want to, but I'm walking." Marne would have been sitting on the passenger side looking out into space. I was operating a Nissan Multi at the time, a reliable car with roadworthy qualities, but light and a bit of a tin can, and limited by a two-wheel-drive transmission. I could comprehend Marne's reluctance, and on that occasion we continued on up the Jesmond road to camp at Riley's Dam.

The view upriver from Cougar Point is somewhat epic; the river, as usual, is a long way down, four thousand vertical feet below, in fact, and from that lofty distance appears forged of metal and seemingly motionless as it winds its way out of the north. The road down is solid, being mostly rock-based, and not unduly narrow, and I manoeuvred the switchbacks easily; I'd done it before. I would not be happy about driving the bottom stretch after heavy rain or runoff, though. Along the clay humps and gullies down there are the only two places ever, in all my years of driving back roads, where, despite my extreme reluctance, I slid off—both times on the mucky uphill side, I'm grateful to note. The downhill side may have the usual drop-off, but moisture drains away more rapidly and it is usually less saturated and less slick. Near the bottom, above that little ranch with the ancient cottonwood-log barn and the old, dirty-white horse looking out the doorway like he owned the place, I'd had to drive around a cow carcass in the middle of the road the first time I went by, years ago. It was a red-and-white Hereford, half eaten and semi-frozen, and partially blocking my way. Something large and furry had dragged it up there, safely out of gunshot range. That cow certainly didn't graze its way uphill in winter snow, patches of which still remained in dark places in the trees.

An hour or two later, after passing High Bar Ranch and the little High Bar Indian Reserve (population two or three) with the standing, plains-style teepee poles for atmosphere, I came to the turnoff to the old Grinder place

The Kostering Ranch house, now a part of the O K Ranch, close to lower Big Bar Creek, circa 1900. Photo courtesy of Don Logan.

above the mouth of Big Bar Creek. I turned up-creek toward the green-stained buildings of the O K Ranch, and turned again just past the ranch, at the big sign with details of the sharp-tailed grouse grassland preservation project in the area, and drove through the gate onto the track to Big Bar Mountain. It was approaching dusk. The first thing I did after I closed the gate was bump into Lawrence Joiner.

He was polite but a bit suspicious—understandably so, given the frequency of vandalism, theft and carelessness in these times. And there are ongoing questions about what constitutes a public road or not. I felt reasonably sure I could be there; Lawrence had other opinions. From where I stood, it was a matter of whose rules we were using. Rather than debate the complexities of the issue, we acquainted ourselves quickly and civilly. He learned I am interested in the history of the area and kindly offered to take me on a tour of the fine open slopes on the southwest side of the mountain. He didn't have to be hospitable but he was, very much so, and I was grateful for it.

Lawrence suggested I park my car, meet his dog, step into his pickup and join them. We talked; among many things, I wanted to know a little of his background, where he came from and why he had chosen this hard, independent ranch life. Turns out Lawrence Joiner grew up in Chilliwack, same as my partner, Marne, though some years earlier. His father ran a mink farm, and her father, Bob Steele, taught Lawrence in high school. "Was he that art teacher?" he asks.

He tells me that he had always known he wanted to ranch and prepared himself accordingly. He took mechanics courses in school and learned how to weld. He knew he would need a wide range of skills to maintain a wide array of farm machinery if he was serious about being a rancher. "Now, it's kind of funny," he says, "I'm the one fixing the broke-down equipment while my cowboys are out there riding the ranges."

The Fraser River looking south from Cougar Point above High Bar. Photo courtesy of Marne St. Claire.

I think of my own father at Darfield, in the spirit of post-war optimism in the late '40s, trying to follow his own dream to make a living as a guide-outfitter. I have a strong memory of him staring out the window, his eyes fixed and glassy, thinking of the endless work and unpaid bills, I imagine, and wondering what his choices were. He had been clearing land down the road from the lodge, a good-sized, still-unfinished log building that he and his former partner, Kori Norgaard, had built, and now, but for Mum, he was on his own. He was cutting and burning brush in early spring and had come up for lunch. The fire got into the root systems of standing fir in a day or two and spread underground, spumes of blue smoke seeping out of the earth at unexpected places down the hillside for weeks.

Now, much of a lifetime later, I find myself haunted at times by the shadows of old settler lives come and gone, a recurrent sense of the struggles and heartaches of our forebearers out here on these new lands; the signs of their hopes, successes and failures are evident most places I go. The sight of derelict log cabin homes tends to make me heartsick. Hints of old memories of my parents' hardships, such as they were, come back to me, and I am impelled to know more of these people that I have glimpsed up here in the half-light of evening on the open slopes of Big Bar Mountain. I have a need to see more clearly where they had chosen to situate their homes, where they had walked and worked and played with their children, and how they came to be here.

Lawrence mentions that Don Logan over at Clinton, a fellow history sleuth who will become a good friend, had taken on the project of interviewing descendants of Big Bar Mountain settlers, chronicling their knowledge and memories, gathering many good copies of old family pictures and, incidentally, but not accidentally, collecting old bottles, relics and other mementos of the period. A number of those found collectibles mark the years when Chinese gold miners were toiling on the already worked-over Fraser River bars, or employed as irrigators, fence builders and cooks at local ranches. As a consequence of his curiosity and hard work, Don has published three indispensable books full of photos and short historic write-ups on the area: *Pioneer Pictures of Big Bar Mountain*, *Dog Creek: 100 Years* and *Canoe Creek BC*.

At some point in the evening's discourse, Lawrence asks me if I'd heard any of the stories about Willie Chisholm, who had lived with his brother Kenny across the Fraser River, down in the rough country by Chisholm Canyon. Harry Marriott, who bought cattle from the Chisholm brothers in 1933 and had stayed with them, was very complimentary, describing them as fine horsemen, capable ranchers, generous and mannerly hosts, but not overly brimming with ambition. Willie was nicknamed "Buffalo Bill" because of the cut of his moustache, his long hair and his tendency to dress the part.

Willie Chisholm liked to go to the socials at the Howling Dog Community Hall on the east side of the Fraser, but on one occasion, as the Big Bar ferry was shut down due to winter ice and snow, he decided to cross, hand over hand, on the ferry cable strung high and tight above the river. He then walked the three or four miles up the creek to the dance. He was bothered, so the story goes, because he got grease from the cable on his "dress clothes." I assume he made the return journey home, probably days later, in the same athletic fashion.

Mike Brundage of the museum at Clinton sent me photocopies of several fine historic pictures of the area. There is one especially intriguing picture of Willie Chisholm and Beulah Madson, third-generation descendant of the original Dugald McDonald family at Watson Bar, standing together in somebody's ranch yard, judging by some stonework, an axe in a chopping block, a bucket, pots, and other homestead paraphernalia in evidence. Beulah was born in 1920 and raised by her grandfather Billy Madson, her mother having run off, so Mike's printed matter states. The story has it that he would place the little child in the shade of a nearby tree close to wherever he was working. Apparently he gave the girl an orphan lamb to look after as an enticement to get her off the bottle. From the same sources, I have it half-figured that Willie and Beulah were related; Jane Ann McDonald from Mount Currie near Pemberton, grandmother to Beulah (and wife of Dugald), was Willie's mother's half-sister. I note that the little cemetery at Watson Bar is referred to as the McDonald-Chisholm cemetery.

The details of the picture are fascinating. Beulah is standing resolutely, arms folded firmly, a wide-brimmed hat set jauntily back on her head. She is wearing what looks like new shoes, shiny, stylish, and overalls, the pant legs a little short. Willie wears a dark frock coat, collar up, with a row of big, bright buttons and newish blue jeans, cuffs turned up in the old cowpoke style in an era when the work pants of choice were likely heavy-duty Cowboy King Denims. His coat is pulled together with a large-buckled belt. He's got the grand moustache; long, greying sideburns; and combed-back, black hair. He must be considerably older than Beulah, if he was adult and selling cattle in 1933. Willie was not a big man, apparently, but he had big work hands, and he stands like a strong man. He would have to be strong to pull himself across the river hand over hand like that.

There is a horse in the background, saddled and bridled. Who is visiting who, and why, I wonder. My guess is it was Willie dropping in on Beulah over at Watson Bar at what was then the McDonald Ranch. He's the one all dressed up with his boots on. She looks like she's just gone in and put on her brand-new, shiny shoes for the event. She stands shorter than Willie. The picture was taken probably in the mid-30s, but Beulah is still alive and feisty, Don Logan informs me, and living at 16 Mile on the Cariboo Highway just north of the Hat Creek turnoff. Her married name is Reaugh; her husband was known as "Kinik"—as in kinikinnick? Kinikinnick

I find myself haunted at times by the shadows of old settler lives come and gone, a recurrent sense of the struggles and heartaches of our forebearers out here on these new lands.

is a common low creeping shrub with red berries and shiny evergreen leaves; the word means "smoking mixture" in an eastern aboriginal language—most likely Cree. There has to be a tale there somewhere.

Lawrence asks if I've heard the Chris Albeitz story. Chris and his wife, Rita, run the ranch down the Fraser River on the west side just upstream from Watson Bar Creek. The Watson Bar area is some of the wildest country anywhere in that West Fraser region. The access out is either via the lengthy Forestry road south to Lillooet or down the long, steep, sandy, sometimes impassable hill to the Big Bar ferry and Big Bar Creek on the east side. I've seen drivers parked, cooling their smoking brakes or steaming radiators, on the little open flat partway down or up. Once, Marne and I watched an older Toyota wagon grinding up the hill past us on a hot, dry day, with two young kids spread-eagled on the hood for traction, and Mum, grim-faced, foot to the floor, blue smoke, heat and dust roiling up behind. We were drinking celebratory gin and tonics at the time, seated in two folding chairs and enjoying the magnificent view up the river north—surely an unexpected and slightly

Beulah Madson of Watson Bar and Willie Chisholm of the Chisholm Ranch above Chisholm Canyon, circa 1936. Photo courtesy of Don Logan.

hallucinatory sight to passersby, rare as they were. Our carefully hoarded ice supply, purchased that morning in Lillooet, was holding out well. Wet or icy weather must stop traffic altogether. That down-hill road would turn into a flume.

One way or another, four or five ranchers scratch out a living in the area. The Albeitzs, whose carefully watered hayfields, a brightly intense green against semi-desert sagebrush-grey, are close to the river, cross to the east side using an outboard-powered aluminum boat they run from a spot near the long-abandoned Watson Bar ferry site.

Watson Bar was a crossing place over the Fraser for the extension north of Lillooet of Governor Douglas's original trail to the gold-fields. If you drive Highway 12 between Lillooet and Pavilion and look carefully across the river, the old trail running along the benches and slopes below the high Forestry road is quite visible from most vantage points. The west-side or "right bank trail," as Judge Begbie named it, was considered to be the best and "most frequented route" north to Big Bar in the early 1860s, before G.B. Wright completed his oddly located wagon road up and over the precipitously steep sides of Carson (Pavilion) Mountain on the east side of the Fraser. South of Watson Bar, the miner's trail is particularly well defined and level, as an improved, hand-dug trail is bound to be, more so than a typical stock or pack trail. But I can spot no obvious sign of it on the west side of the river north of Watson

Bar. In contrast to the sagebrush benches on the east side, the steep stone walls around Chisholm Canyon upriver would have made for tough trail making. A trail further north must have veered up over the rocky hump away from the river and come out close to the Big Bar ferry site.

Marne and I met Mrs. Albeitz, briefly, three or four years earlier. We were having a bunwich lunch, folding chairs out and set up at the side of the High Bar road overlooking the river. We were focused on getting a clear look at some fly-chasing Lewis woodpeckers, rare in these parts and attractive, on and around a pine snag below us, when along comes Rita in a pickup. She stopped to say hello, perhaps glad to talk for a few minutes or maybe just to check us out. I had been prowling around with binoculars, spotting birds here and there, and the sunlight may have glinted off my lenses. She had crossed the river in the usual manner and was on her way to make phone calls at the Big Bar school, some considerable distance up the draw; she told us she had a lot of backed-up business to cover.

Lawrence Joiner tells me that she has attained some renown locally for her dedication to delivering her kids to school in that tin shell of a boat across the river, on time, every day. This is the Fraser River, you understand, massive, powerful, rough, fast, sometimes in flood, always muddy, and at times plugged with snags and deadheads. "She never misses a day," he says.

I think out loud that I guess she must carry a spare motor. Lawrence says not so. In fact, when he crossed with them one time, the couple chuckled when he loosened the tops of his work boots, worried that he might need to kick them off in a hurry.

Lawrence proceeds to tell me about Chris Albeitz and his famous winter swim. Chris is Australian and apparently tough—rugged—as many Australians are reputed to be. Around Christmas some years back, so the now-fabled story goes, the couple made arrangements with the caretaker of the High Bar Ranch, downriver on the east side, to meet them at a certain time in order to transport them across to some festive event. He never showed. It was dark and cold, about twenty degrees of freezing below Fahrenheit. They waited. Finally, impatient, and probably keen for a party,

Chris took off his boots and most of his clothes and swam across, angling downstream to the other side. His plan, apparently, was to trot quickly down to the ranch house to give the man's memory a kick, and maybe warm up a bit before he froze solid. Sounds like a sort of "Down Under" thing to do, to me. Well, he made it there alright, but he did allow that he was starting to stiffen up some. He could see a light in the window, and when he came up to it and looked in, he saw the gentleman in question passed out, face down on the kitchen table, an empty booze bottle in front of him. "I was so mad I could have killed him," Chris Albeitz is supposed to have recounted later, "but I was too damned cold."

THE NEXT DAY, LAWRENCE IS OFF AS THE SUN RISES, WORK BOUND, HIS FAITH-ful doggy partner Zipper beside him, roaring out of the O K Ranch yard, headed for the slopes of Big Bar Mountain. After a quick cup of coffee and an orange, I am similarly hustling a few minutes later, on my way to Grinder Creek. There is no time like the cool light of dawn.

I leave a note of thanks on Lawrence's door. He tells a good story, and I'm grateful to him for that and for generously touring me around parts of Big Bar Mountain that evening. I especially appreciated hearing his observations and thoughts on homesteaders' lives in an older, harder era. He and I may not meet again, but who can foresee the country we'll walk or ride, the rivers we'll cross, the occasional mountain we'll climb, the still, quiet places we'll come to. Lawrence Joiner is a classic Cariboo rancher, competent and cut from tough old-time material, and I've been privileged to spend time with him. May we all walk well.

ON THE WAY TO GRINDER CREEK

All the way to heaven is heaven.
—St. Catherine of Siena

I PICK MY WAY DOWN OFF THE STEEP, GRASS-SLOPED ESKER ONTO THE OLD wagon track. In front of me, two or three mule deer drift silently into misty standing timber, seeming not to move among the shadowy tree trunks. It is early May and I am walking west up Grinder Creek above the Empire Valley Ranch headquarters, on the lookout for the old-time Grinder and Zimmerlee homesteads farther along the way. I'm not exactly certain what I'm after, but I'm confident I'll find signs of the old places somewhere ahead in this narrow, shallow little valley. The track ends five miles farther up the slope at the site of a late-nineteenth-century grist mill, just below the outlet of what used to be called China Lake. I'm scanning the wooded slope on my left for hand-sawed or chopped fir and pine stumps of a certain size and age, approximately 110 years old, and typically spring-cut and sap-extruded. Such sign would indicate that somebody, possibly Phil Grinder himself or one of his sons—Johnny, his oldest, maybe—was cutting cabin logs here a long time ago.

The creek running down through a willow, cottonwood and poplar bottom on my right is not immediately visible, but I hear its early runoff gurgle. It sounds excited. Bright orange and red willow stems and pale poplar trunks pierce this drizzly spring light. Leaves have not yet unfurled, but willow buds are thickening and the ground is dank with humus; snow is not long gone from this valley. A light fog gathers in the damp along the creek bottom.

After a short mile, telltale stumps of the right cabin-sized diameter appear, old, chopped, mossy, but still firm. Wood keeps well in this dry country, frequently sun-parched or frozen, and I'm thinking the Grinder cabin site must be near. The track veers closer to the creek, and through the brush and cottonwood trunks I spot a set of elderly hay corrals, and fields opening on the far side. I examine the corrals later and see punky fence logs and a great buildup of old dry manure and chaff in the corners, indicative of long use. A small pile of not-so-old fence poles has been stacked to cure beside the track ahead of me.

There is something about the view that does not fit; the grassy ground past the logs seems unnaturally, almost imperceptibly, disturbed. It's too flat. The natural micro-contours are not there. As I draw closer for a careful look, slight, straight rows of lightly heaped, rotted red earth the colour of fir wood, culminating in ninety-degree angles, the last hints of floor joists and house corners, present themselves, unmistakably, as a cabin layout approximately twenty feet long. All other signs of the cabin structure have disappeared. Behind, on the bank edge above the creek bottom beside red willow brush, are hints of aged wood residue through last year's matted grass, signs of the woodpile perhaps, reduced to earth. There is a grassy hole in the ground, a privy hole, down-creek from the house site. A ditch snakes along the edge of the north-facing slope from upstream; whoever lived here had irrigated this little clearing, likely for a kitchen garden. I would have missed most detail if the new grass had begun to green.

At my feet, on either side of where the door of the cabin would have been, standing out from all around them in their own stunted way, are two rhubarb plants. They have struggled out of the ground for one more season, but their stalks are wizened and wan. If these plants are as elderly as I think they are, a century old at least, quite long enough to have thoroughly drained their earth of nutrients, they have earned the right to be fragile and pale. These little beauties might well be among the oldest living rhubarb plants in British Columbia. Their diminished note of scurvy-avoiding domesticity clinches it for me; this has to be the Grinder place. I am reasonably certain that by the mid-1890s a Grinder had claimed but not finalized the pre-emption of these meadows on lower Grinder Creek. They are part of what is now called Grinder Field, as delineated on one of the maps in the Churn Creek Protected Area Management Plan. There were new pre-emptions and settlement elsewhere around Empire Valley in that same period, no doubt due to the access provided by the inception of the ferry across the Fraser at the mouth of Churn Creek in 1890. Grinder's unrecorded claim suggests his stay there was short, if he stayed at all. Logic, the probable timing of it, and e-mail and phone discussions with Chilco Choate over at Gaspard Lake, and with Mike Brundage and Don Logan, both associated with the Clinton Museum at the time, suggest it was likely old Phil himself, on a brief land investment venture perhaps, before retreating back across to his home territory around Big Bar Creek. Who else could it be? Why else would the creek and meadows have come to carry the Grinder name? Unfortunately the few written references to a Grinder here in Empire Valley never include a first name.

A chance meeting and discussion later at the Empire Valley calving barn with Phil Pigeon, an affable horseman from Meadow Lake near Clinton, provided some further confirmation. It turns out Phil is a great-grandson of old Phil G. In fact, he is the old-timer's namesake, and he was sure, given the timing, that it was his famous ancestor, and not a younger relative, who temporarily claimed this piece of accessible, fertile, but not expansive, bottomland up Grinder Creek. Most of the good land around Empire Valley was claimed or inhabited early.

I admire the sheer oldness of it all—though nothing in contrast to the Old World, of course—and I'm intrigued by the uncertainties and questions, and the intrinsically unfinished and shifting nature of the process of asking and learning. History, that is to say our collective memories of ourselves, fades so resolutely, so quickly, into the forgotten past, and we are rendered more foolish and ineffective without that knowledge of who we are, where we came from, what we did, and where we lived. Imagine attempting to live

Phil Grinder, co-founder of Alkali Lake Ranch, and Nancy (nee Kala'llst), his wife of long standing. Mr. Grinder died in 1915. Photo courtesy of Don Logan.

without memory, yet our current age, immersed in the short digital present, seems to encourage that. I understand a bit more why many older cultures work so hard to preserve their memories; they are preserving who they are. Without our deepest sense of history, identity and place, we lose the contexts so necessary for intelligent choices and actions; without context, meaning is reduced or lost. Impulse is a poor substitute for thought.

I button up my coat and continue on in the drizzle, grateful I'm not walking in thick, wet brush. I will be looking for the Zimmerlee place farther up the draw. Past the Grinder cabin site, the track crosses the creek and comes out at the lower end of a long, open hayfield, just above the old hay corrals. A narrow riparian strip, more willow brush and poplars, extends along the creek for a stretch before widening into a cottonwood flat up the valley. The fog is settling and a few ghostly black Angus cows graze in and out of visibility. I had heard one of them bawling earlier across the creek, a protracted plea of some bovine kind, the sound muffled and small, directionless and echoless, in the mist.

Forty years ago in England, the land of my ancestors, I took a country bus from Salisbury in Wiltshire to see Stonehenge. I made a wrong stop and had to walk back two or three miles on a winding side road through the cold and fog to reach the place. It was February. My visual world was without colour: black-and-white Holstein cows grazing and moving slowly about; single, large, leafless oak trees outlined against dense white fog; barrows, long, low, prehistoric earth mounds, ancient living or worshipping places, a series of them; and small groups of black rooks, conversing and arguing in their classically corvid manner. The fog drifts. The rooks' low squabble shifts in and out of my consciousness, and cows and birds move in and out of sight. Up ahead, the circled stone monoliths loom, step by step, into view, the mists moving slowly around them, their vertical presence accentuated by lack of physical context, excepting the disappearing road and the fog's opacity. There is virtually no car traffic. I am alone, walking to Stonehenge.

Now I am alone walking up Grinder Creek. On top of the bald, south-facing slopes above and behind me on my right is an area I know to be the old Empire Valley Ranch "dry farm." I had prowled around up there one spring earlier, looking to see where old-timers had attempted to grow wheat without irrigation a century or more earlier (hence the former grist mill up in the bush at track's end). I had seen an expanse of cleared land, then hints of old furrow rows, field edges, fence lines and a long, narrow row of scraggly fir trees growing along a disintegrated snake fence on what I think was a property line. That fence must have stopped snow and fallen cones long enough to hold moisture for germination once upon a time. A flock of unusually low-elevation Clark's nutcrackers was using one fir snag as a base for eyeing me and the world, and haranguing each other. There is evidently no peace in nutcracker world. They miss little and pass up nothing. These noisy birds must have been in migration to higher places.

I come to an antique wood and steel binder parked, as if deliberately, between the track and another grassed-in irrigation ditch running along the high side of the field. The machine looks almost new, even though it would have sat there in its grass clump for years. Its presence attests to the need for bread and the practice of wheat farming in this remote land in the old days. There are still hints of paint on the metal parts, and finish on the wood. It is a much more complex piece of machinery than the simple horse-drawn hay mowers and rakes I remember from my young, post-war days up the North Thompson River. My friend Ken Schilling of Darfield, who collects antique farm machinery, would surely pine to see this one. He has a yard and large shed full of old farming and logging relics, large and small, including an old one-stroke engine with a heavy flywheel the size of a locomotive wheel that you turn with hernia-inducing vigour to initiate its wheezy start.

A little farther up the hill I cross a fence line, which I assume separates the original Grinder from the later Zimmerlee holdings. The irrigation ditch crosses at the same spot. I look hard for signs of an old home-place there but find nothing. What I do notice are three finely axed, squared and thoroughly seasoned fir timbers, used as culvert logs over the now dry and grassed-in ditch. Nobody goes to that trouble for a culvert. These are surely old house logs, likely from Zimmerlee's place up the valley. The axe man, probably Mr. Zimmerlee himself, had sure control of his tools. People took time to do quality log work as a matter of course in those earlier days.

I don't mind a little alarm in a startled omnivore, close at hand.

The fog is lifting slowly. I carry on. The valley narrows. The upper meadow is not large, and I come soon to the top end of that long cottonwood and poplar grove close to the creek. Along the edge are piles of rotted log chunks and notched fence-rail ends, what's left of a long oval corral or small pasture, recently pulled together to burn. Those crumbling fence logs were originally large, straight, mostly knotless Douglas fir. I have a growing impression that the oldest fences in this country were frequently built of really big timber, in spite of the obviously heavy labour necessary. Perhaps old-time horses were more determined in their need to escape then, and the cattle tougher; certainly some were larger and wilder if the stories of Stranger Wycott's massive, long-horned steers running feral up Churn Creek are an indicator.

I come round a brushy corner and scare up a black bear snuffling around a young dandelion patch. He takes off like an Olympic sprinter. That fella knows all about firearm range, and he's getting out of it. We are, after all, in cow and cowboy land. I like his cautious attitude; I don't mind a little alarm in a startled omnivore, close at hand. My friend Warren Menhinick, over at Gold Bridge, says, "Always remember, John, you can't out-wrestle a bear," as if I need the hint. Then he adds, "But sometimes your number is up." He's a droll lad, that Warren. I've seen countless black bears in my life, starting at age two, and they have always, but for three exceptions, run, walked or ambled away; those three other times, it was me doing the walking and talking. I can hear this current bear in full survival mode, thundering across the creek and up a bank through brush on the other side. A couple of irritated ravens up-creek fly out in a chorus of curses, and cattle on the flat up on top sound the alarm.

The sun is out, warm on my face, as I reach the top end of that disintegrating corral: time to stop, rest and be grateful, look around and have a snack. There are certain interesting clues around me: more freshly disturbed old corral log bits in small piles, a well-worn creek crossing on my left, the ditch running below an old fence on my right. And between them a low, levelled, rectangular earth platform, edged with carefully placed creek stones of a uniformly large size: an obvious building site. James and Maggie Zimmerlee's house, I presume. There are two or three photographs in the Clinton museum purporting to be of their garden here, up Grinder Creek, that include some of this same fine view, little changed, down the valley. The garden looked lush, but good soil and a beautiful vista are no antidote for isolation. Don Logan, in his book on the Big Bar Mountain settlers, quotes Maggie, in a letter, stating she is tired from all those long days seeding the garden and washing clothes, and that she feels "awful lonesome" since her neighbour and friend Mrs. Jim Bishop, down by Brown Lake, left the valley with her family to resettle closer to Clinton.

There are no vestiges of house logs at the upper place now, not a scrap. In earlier times, well-shaped and preserved house timbers would have been a valuable commodity, easily recycled. I notice the ditch is unusually shallow and wide above the house, as if that was where stock watered, or where wagons with sacks of grain to be ground at China Lake crossed. The bottom there is gravelled, unlike any other section. The old wagon track to the grist mill appears to have run right by the Zimmerlee home; the family would have been glad of the distraction and occasional company. I picture their big kitchen garden below that ditch, and I'm still thinking of the size

James and Margaret Zimmerlee circa 1914, from California by wagon. They and their large family settled at Empire Valley, moving later to Big Bar Creek. Photo courtesy of Don Logan.

of those fence logs. It would have taken several strong bodies to lift them. Those Zimmerlee kids must have grown up skookum.

In her letter, Maggie comments on the hard work her husband had to do to construct the ditch so it would hold its water. The ground was too porous, and she notes that her husband had to bring in "other stuff," probably clay, to do the job. "Zim was a tough old snoozer," said Harry Marriott in *Cariboo Cowboy*, citing the couple as fine examples of the self-reliant pioneers who Europeanized the North American West. The family had come north from California in a covered wagon drawn by four horses, working for cash here and there along the way, and taking two years to finally reach Empire Valley. Eventually the family, like Phil Grinder earlier, moved over to lower Big Bar Creek across the Fraser, where Zimmerlee farmed and worked on the Big Bar Mountain cattle range, and where there were more neighbours. Like Grinder, the Zimmerlees did not go through the formality of pre-empting their place up Grinder Creek.

The family was drawn here originally by the promise of free land. Someone from Empire Valley, Jim Bishop the story has it, happened to be in Ashcroft when Mr. and Mrs. Zimmerlee and their clutch of children were passing through. Bishop suggested the family move up to Empire Valley to augment the youthful population so that a school might be opened. Bishop and his wife, Ann, had their own children in need of education. The Zimmerlees agreed and the school was built a bit later, around 1912, above the little dam on Koster Creek, just below Brown Lake. Its existence was short. The scant remains of that place of learning—a few scattered nails and wood scraps on a tiny flat beside the road—are still faintly visible. I find it slightly unnerving, and a touch ghostlike, to picture the two or three rows of motley little would-be scholars, tending, I'm guessing, toward the scruffy, seated a hundred years ago in that space on that level piece of ground where now there is nothing.

I have a copy of a photograph of what must have been parents' day at the school probably late in the 1912/1913 year. The class would have been composed mainly of Bishop and Zimmerlee children. Everybody's dressed up in their best clean clothes; the women wear bright white blouses, and Billy and Tommy Boyle stand firmly in the back row in ties and cowboy hats. They were raised on the ranch across the road from the school. Harry Higgenbottom, husband of Mariah Wycott and father of Annie Grinder, stands between the Boyle brothers. The schoolmarm, Bessie Sims, is seated on a saddled horse (which you can just discern if you look very carefully).

When they first moved to Empire Valley, the Zimmerlee family lived in a cabin on a bleak north-facing slope by Brown Lake, across from the lower end of Bishop's field; they later moved up Grinder Creek to live on their new land. The first place, previously lived in by one of the Bishop families, must surely have been dark and cold in winter (though it was close to the just-built school). Now a single post and a caved-in root cellar hole at the bottom of the slope behind remain to show that families once resided in this place. A few Zimmerlee descendants continue to live around the region. Others moved back south as far as Oregon.

That must have been quite a walk for the Zimmerlee kids, about three miles from their new home up Grinder Creek to school each day, rain or shine or snow. As a six-, seven-, and eight-year-old at Darfield in the late 1940s, I spent my first educational years in a one-room, eight-grade schoolhouse not unlike Empire Valley School. It came complete with a barrel wood stove, woodshed, outdoor privy and lean-to shed behind for Lucille Evans's horse. When the temperature dropped, we pulled our desks close in around the hot stove to stay warm. And I walked a similar distance back and forth to school. I remember pumping my little stumps as hard as I could up that hillside to reach home before dark. In a world of winter snow, the light from the coal oil lamp in our kitchen window up the hill above me was a bright and warming sight.

Sometimes I wonder if it is possible to sense the spiritual, that is to say subtle, residue of sentient beings, human or otherwise—those little students in those small schoolhouses, for example—after they have spent extended time in a particular space or place. What is it that they leave behind? Some sort of shadow? Do we in some way walk through them when we are there?

I sit, eating my crackers and cheese, absorbing the sun, admiring the fine view, remembering, pondering. My thoughts turn, as they are bound, to Phil Grinder, who may have lived a brief portion of his long lifespan, over a century ago, down the valley from where I am sitting so pleasantly now. There are Grinder descendants throughout the South Cariboo, and the Grinder name comes up frequently. The founder of the dynasty, Phil Grinder, was a small man, not heavily built, wiry, energetic and not lacking in intelligence, it seems. But while he carried out a variety of business transactions throughout his busy life, Grinder signed his name with an X. He began his Cariboo life early in the rush, panning for gold, but caught on quickly that a steady livelihood could be earned packing for gold seekers over the long roads between Lillooet, Yale and Barkerville. Like other packers, his peer William Wycott for example, he realized he needed low-elevation land along the Fraser River to winter his stock, so he took up land on Grinder Flats, near the bottom of Big Bar Creek, in the summer of 1868.

At some time over those years he got together with Nancy Kalest (Kala'llst), from Alkali Lake, apparently, but part of an old Secwepemc (Shuswap) family from the Gaspard Creek country west of the Fraser, and together they raised a large family. Their first child, Johnny, was born in 1872. Harry Marriott asserts that Phil and Nancy "were respected and liked by all." Don Logan has shown me a couple of copies of old photos of Nancy; in one she is clearly

Parents' day at Empire Valley School circa 1912–13. That's the teacher, Bessie Sims, in the back on the left. Photo courtesy of Don Logan.

into her later years, but she's wearing her best riding duds, is mounted on a good horse and looks strong and full of fire. I have to believe she could look after herself. Like her husband, Nancy was not tall, but then few were in those times. Their grandsons Henry and Albert Grinder were highly regarded cowboys, and there are others in the family, Henry's sons, for example, who became known for their ranching, rodeo and woods competence.

Phil Grinder was renowned as a witty fellow and appears to have had a good sense of fun. Fans of local Cariboo history tell a stock set of stories about him. In *Tales from the Ranches*, Harry Marriott recounts one about a time when Phil, who was not loath to celebrate whatever there was to celebrate, was staying and socializing over at the Clinton hotel. Late one night and unable to "pry a window open," as Marriott puts it, but feeling an urgent nighttime need, Grinder made use of an Englishman's fine riding boot as a urinal. It was handy and empty. We can just imagine that gentleman's spluttering response the morning after. "You don't really take it too hard, do you, Stranger?" Grinder is supposed to have responded. Then there was the time another traveller, an Englishman of course, partaking of the hospitality at the Grinder ranch, enquires as to the location of the lavatory. Phil points out the door and says, "There's 160 acres out there, partner. You're welcome to use any part of it." So often it seems these sorts of stories are told at the expense of some well-dressed, high-tone English gent or other with some cash and pretensions to social elevation, out for a jaunt in the colonies.

Marriott tells another tale from the time when Grinder ran the ferry on the river at Big Bar—just a rowboat in those early days before reaction ferries—and a man named Barney O'Rourke wanted to cross. It just so happened it was Election Day, and the Irishman, a staunch Sinn Feiner and liberal who hated anything that even hinted at Englishness, was on his way to vote. The incumbent, on the other hand, was not only an old established conservative who had represented the local riding for years and had given Phil his ferry job, but was also the Clinton storekeeper to whom Phil owed money. Grinder was doubly in debt. "Go around," he yelled, "go around," knowing full well O'Rourke would have many miles to go any other way, north or south, and would surely miss his chance to cast his ballot. Phil Grinder, that old Pennsylvania "Deutsch" man, was a character, all right, but while there are more good Grinder stories to relate, hard facts about him are difficult to find.

There is the question of Phil Grinder's probable initial connection to the original Alkali Lake Ranch located in an exceptionally rich and beautiful valley up off the Fraser River north of Dog Creek. Many have stated it was the first ranch, or at least the first registered ranch, in the Cariboo, or even all of British Columbia, and that it was Herbert Bowe who pre-empted it in 1861. Most, including the authoritative Branwen Patenaude in *Trails to Gold*, part of her Cariboo roadhouse series, confirm that Bowe had a partner in that venture, namely Phil Grinder. That Alkali Lake partnership did not last long, although Patenaude notes that Bowe and Grinder, together with several other partners, developed a ranch and two-storey log roadhouse called

Mountain House at what is now Jesmond on the stagecoach route between Kelly Lake and Dog Creek. Mountain House was later owned by several generations of the Coldwell family. But just how strong is the claim that the Alkali Lake Ranch was the first in the Cariboo?

HISTORY, I AM LEARNING, IS NEVER SIMPLE. IN FACT, THERE IS SOMETHING increasingly mirage-like about the results of my own small efforts to nail down details of early BC ranching history. Everyone has an opinion, usually firmly if not rigidly held, not least about the correctness of their particular viewpoint. And there are more subtle underlying perspectives, especially as regards the poor and powerless, the unschooled, the culturally different and newcomers. Written records are limited and are sometimes wildly variable and contradictory. At times, differing versions of a story pitch family against family. Detailed knowledge is usually local, not broad in scope, and so much depends on the volume and the accent of the voice of the person doing the telling. The more I try to ascertain the basic facts of Cariboo ranching, for example, the more I learn that assumptions are often made, not checked, and eventually taken to be God's truth itself. We all do it. Academia, on the other hand, under the guise of objectivity, tends to focus more on large context, abstract concepts and accuracy, if possible, but not on the specifics of place and the lively personal detail and feeling that make much local history so interesting. Accordingly, then, there are a number of nominees for the admittedly arbitrary, and ultimately unimportant, "first rancher" honours in the Cariboo-Chilcotin.

Some have said it was Jerome and Thaddeus Harper, presumed founders of the mighty Gang Ranch, who arrived here just ahead of the American not-so-civil war (1861–65). But their first holdings in British Columbia, among them the Harper Ranch east of Kamloops on the South Thompson River (itself a possibility, perhaps, as the first ranch in BC), and the Perry Ranch down by Cache Creek, are well out of the Cariboo area. And the gate at the Gang Ranch headquarters on lower Gaspard Creek in the East Chilcotin says "est. 1865" (if we are to believe it). The brothers were reportedly gathering cattle in Oregon for a drive to Barkerville in 1862, but where were

Alkali Lake Ranch headquarters, founded by Herbert Bowe and Phil Grinder in 1861. Photo courtesy of Marne St. Claire.

they headquartered? They were certainly doing business all around what is now southwestern and central BC, including sawmilling at Yale and Quesnel, flour-milling at the mouth of the Bonaparte River outside of Ashcroft, and investing in a slaughterhouse near Barkerville, not to mention their various mining enterprises, during those early years.

Clinton historian Don Logan, in his careful examination of pre-emption records, informs us that, contrary to common folklore, Thaddeus Harper did not actually pre-empt land in the remote Gaspard Creek basin west of the Fraser until 1883, and there were no Gang Ranch buildings constructed there before that time. By then brother Jerome was long dead (1874). It is not illogical to assume an earlier founding date, given that ex-miners and would-be settlers in numbers were searching out good land in the wake of the gold rush; however, most of those efforts were on the east, and much more accessible, side of the Fraser River. I did a quick check of the most pertinent but non-primary-sourced Cariboo history books in my own library, and so far, while some writers imply early ownership, I have discovered no source that states clear, emphatic founding dates for the Gaspard Creek holdings before 1883. Therefore, as Don strongly suggests, any dates in the 1860s that we may hear are likely only guesses, wishful thinking, unchecked assumptions— or else they apply to the Harpers' varied properties and investments at large. And Thaddeus Harper founded the mighty Gang Ranch all on his own. The brothers, most especially Thaddeus, do deserve recognition, long overdue, for some of the longest (in time and distance), most difficult cattle drives in North American history, including one, apparently, that went all the way to San Francisco via a roundabout route through Salt Lake City in Utah. Their original intentions, it is said, had been to drive all the way to Chicago.

A further suggestion for "first rancher" has been Robert Carson, whose ranch was on the early gold road up over Carson (Pavilion) Mountain from Lillooet, but Branwen Patenaude's careful research puts that illusion to rest. Carson did not pre-empt until 1867, although the route up the hillside past his place was dotted briefly with roadhouses to serve gold rushers, who were no doubt too exhausted and distracted to notice the views east of some of the more attractive grazing land imaginable on the rolling, poplar-groved, south-facing slopes of the mountain. Patenaude makes a tantalizing reference in *Trails to Gold* to "Martley's ranch" located at the foot of Carson Mountain in 1858–59, but the owner did not pre-empt until 1861, and the enterprise seems to have been more of a roadhouse and farm than a ranch.

Another early rancher option, referred to by Patenaude and also by Diana French in her book *Ranchland*, is the famous, or infamous, ex-Hudson's Bay Company man Donald McLean, father to the truly infamous McLean boys (three of whom, plus Alex Hare, ran amuck south of Kamloops in 1879, killing two men in separate, senseless incidents in the vicinity of Brigade Lake. After a siege of their hideout, a cabin at Douglas Lake on what is now Spaxomin Reserve, the brothers were arrested, imprisoned, found guilty and hung). McLean Sr. pre-empted land around the mouth of Hat Creek, north of Cache Creek, in 1861 and ran a ranch and roadhouse there in the early 1860s. It is now a provincially operated heritage site and tourist attraction. Donald McLean, who had a reputation for cruelty to aboriginal people from his Hudson's Bay Company (HBC) days, was eventually shot—some might say assassinated—in the last episode of the Chilcotin War in 1864.

Tom Carolan, quoted in Veera Bonner's *Chilcotin: Preserving Pioneer Memories*, bluntly states his choice for "first rancher" honours: "[Raphael] Valenzuela, the first rancher in the Cariboo." And again in *Tales of the Ranches* he declares that Valenzuela, originally a pack-train man, "was the first one...to bring cattle in." He ranged his stock, apparently, around Dog Creek, and there is a Valenzuela Lake and a Valenzuela Creek draining into Meadow Lake on higher ground farther east that may well have been part of his summer grazing range.

Mule- and horse-train men, frequently Spanish American, were packing for the HBC from Forts Okanogan and Vancouver down on the Columbia River, and from Fort Thompson (Kamloops), north to Fort Alexandria as far back as the 1820s. Fort Alexandria, a supply post on the Fraser River in the northern Cariboo, south of present-day Quesnel, was founded in 1821. In *The History of the Northern Interior of British Columbia*, Father A.G. Morice reports a famously heavy winterkill of animals in 1826 that specifically included the Fort Alexandria horse herd; in other words, there was HBC domestic stock that far up the Fraser that early. Some of the Company's packers, including Valenzuela and several fellow Hispanics, wintered their stock in the low-elevation Dog Creek area and around Clinton, and had done so for years. Branwen Patenaude refers to a ranch just outside Clinton, known today as the Spanish Ranch, that was used by packers as a relay station "dating back to pre-gold-rush times."

Patenaude, Irene Stangoe, and Hilary Place, who wrote *Dog Creek*, all indicate in their various ways that Valenzuela's ranch may have predated the start of the gold rush (1858). Irene Stangoe, in *Cariboo-Chilcotin: Pioneer People and Places*, is of the opinion that he homesteaded and wintered there for almost thirty years. She and Place both say he built his main building there, later to become part of Dog Creek House, before 1860. Valenzuela's daughter Placida claimed 1856 to be the year of its construction.

So a good, but far from certain, case does exist for the Spanish-speaking Raphael Valenzuela as the first rancher in the Cariboo and perhaps even British Columbia. But now that we are pushing the bounds of historical curiosity and conjecture, there is another equally intriguing and even wilder— some might say farfetched—possibility. Some of the very first stock raisers in British Columbia, and conceivably in all of northwestern North America, notwithstanding the early presence of the HBC, may well have been aboriginal individuals here in BC: Secwepemc (Shuswap), Nlaka'pamux (Thompson) or Okanagan, most likely. The Company is known to have moved cattle from Fort Vancouver to Fort Kamloops and points farther north at least as early as 1840. Robert Belyk, in his book on HBC chief trader John Tod, reports a small herd of cattle at Fort Alexandria in 1841.

At a barbecue at the Menhinicks' place outside of Gold Bridge some time back, the cowboy poet, history buff, impresario and rancher Mike Puhallo out of Kamloops, now deceased, suggested the Indian "first rancher" theory to me, and we kicked it around for part of an evening. We did agree there was a certain irony in the idea. While the HBC was carrying out its fur business in BC in relative peace, the process of colonization and settlement of the American West was marked by wars and disruption throughout much of what are now the states of Washington, Oregon, Idaho and Montana. The Whitman massacre was in 1847, the battle of the Little Bighorn in 1876, the courageous and bloody Nez Perce retreat east and north toward the Canadian territories under Chief Joseph, Looking Glass and White Bird took place in 1877. Western Montana was lawless. American settlement and ranching beyond the purview of the forts and trading posts could not occur at a significant rate until the early or mid-1880s. Except for the Willamette Valley in Oregon, perhaps, ranching in BC got, at minimum, a twenty-five-year head start on the ranches of the US northwest.

Significant portions of the interior of south-central British Columbia are well-watered, low-elevation, open grasslands and fir, lodgepole and ponderosa pine parklands, country well suited to the raising of domestic stock. The indigenous peoples lived mainly along or close to the three major drainages: the Fraser, the Thompson (North and South) and the Okanagan Rivers, all rich salmon rivers until modern times, and all running through those same grass and parklands. The country was and still is ecologically diverse and rich in food sources and would have supported large aboriginal populations. Those pre-contact cultures were relatively sedentary, complex and varyingly hierarchical. The huge pithouse village site at Keatley Creek, up off the Fraser River south of Pavilion in nearby St'at'imc (Lillooet) territory, which was thoroughly examined by archaeologist Brian Hayden and associates over many years, demonstrates heavy prehistoric population density and vertical social structure in ancient times very convincingly. The scope of the site at Keatley Creek, the variations in sizes of the former pithouse homes, and the range of diversity and quantity of food deposits on living floors indicate a wide spectrum of affluence from rich to near starvation. Some of the kekuli (pithouse) holes there are huge, the largest by far that I have seen. It seems to me entirely natural that certain wealthy and powerful individuals and/or families in early post-contact times would have quickly seen the benefits of stock ownership, of both horses and cattle, and traded for themselves accordingly. Chiefs Paul and Tranquille in the Kamloops area and Chief Nicola from Douglas Lake come to mind as possible examples. Chief William from the Williams Lake area is another.

Certainly, beginning with the very first ranches and cattle drives in the region, southern British Columbia is unique for its regular employment of Indian cowboys. Probably because of precedents set over many years by the fur companies, who hired aboriginal labour at their fur posts as a matter of necessity, the main issue for early BC cattlemen in a worker-short world was whether skilled, country-wise horsemen were available, irrespective of their culture or origins. Most aboriginal men were tough, competent and steady workers, as were the women, and many would have had prior experience with horses. The issue of race, in this context, was not so important. And north of the 49th parallel, armed conflict between Europeans and aboriginals had been relatively limited.

Donald McLean's house behind an historic hotel building at Hat Creek Ranch. It was first located across the Bonaparte River on the east side close to where the Cariboo Highway is now. Photo courtesy of Marne St. Claire.

The existence of Indian cowboys, and their familiarity with most facets of owning and using horses, raises interesting questions about whether there were horses, and especially wild horses, in the Cariboo-Chilcotin region before the arrival locally of the first Europeans. Simon Fraser's observations on his epic 1808 trip down the great river named after him answer the first part of that question in a cautious affirmative: domesticated horses, or signs of their use, were occasionally seen, especially downriver. There seem not to have been large numbers in early post-contact days, according to the quite specific estimates of the authoritative ethnographer James Teit of Spences Bridge, who did his documentations around the turn of the twentieth century. Teit's Secwepemc informants told him that horses were not plentiful in their territory until about 1840 and were first introduced to the northern Secwepemc by trade in about 1830. If this is true, the likelihood of horses, tame or wild, away from the Fraser River in adjacent, higher-elevation, more forested backcountry would have been limited.

The journalist Paul St. Pierre corroborates this view in a discussion with Gabriel (Gay) Bayliff in *Chilcotin Holiday*, a collection of his newspaper

Prehistoric pithouse village site at Keatley Creek. Note the large size of some of the kekuli holes. Photo courtesy of John Schreiber.

articles. Gay quotes his father Hugh, an early Chilcotin rancher, stating that as recently as the 1880s the Tsilhqot'in people out west, particularly away from the Fraser River, had no horses, and there was no word in their language then for "horse."

James Teit remarks, incidentally, that in the beginning, horses were used extensively for food. He is not alone in that assertion. Teit, who worked for and with the great anthropologist Franz Boas, was highly regarded by all who knew him, native and non-native. He was facile with languages and could converse easily with his Nlaka'pamux relatives by marriage, and with his neighbours and workmates. His proficiency with local dialects and with the related Secwepemc and St'at'imc languages was vital for his ethnographic and Nlaka'pamux land claims activities.

As to the pre-contact presence of wild horses, some say yes, others no. The HBC, the packers and, later, the early ranchers were bringing large numbers of horses into the region by the 1850s at the latest and, as previously stated, the HBC was using horses at Fort Alexandria in the early 1820s. Horses go feral easily, and the presence of wild horses in the backcountry in modern times proves nothing, especially as local ranchers, from the earliest times, have had horses run off as a matter of course. Teit conversed at length with, and wrote about, Salishan-speaking aboriginal peoples on both sides of the US border as far east as western Montana. He suggests that horses along the Fraser River were obtained in trade via the Okanagans from aboriginal groups south of the American border: the Sanpoil, Spokane, Coeur d'Alene and Flathead, for example. Other sources might include Sahaptin-speaking Yakima, Cayuse and Nez Perce horse traders farther south.

There is another kind of history emanating from this country and presenting itself to us as myth stories and legends: the ancient aboriginal tales from pre-contact times, of course, and other, more recent, myth stories emerging now as we settler newcomers find our paths and places in this new world. These stories have a sense of the timeless and a larger-than-life quality about them. Many of them are about tough times and places: the first horses and horsemen; the old hunters, trappers and packers; the first ranchers; their wives and daughters on the home front; the tough old settler days and tough old folks like Phil Grinder and Stranger Wycott; heroes and heroines; young outlaws with wild blood, grievances and no place to go; not to mention cold winters, floods, wildfires, isolation and loneliness. These subjects and many more morph into legend and myth as the stories continue to be told and retold. The process of mythologizing is relentless, enduring and wild, and we are all part of it.

I gather myself to move on. I do a fast dance over the rocks at the old creek crossing to avoid wet feet, and in so doing raise the conversational pitch of that pair of ravens in the cottonwood jungle downstream. They are clearly investigating something important. They rise up indignantly as I pass on up to the grassy alkaline flats to the south. My return route will be slightly circuitous; there is a historic wagon track continuing south towards Lone Cabin Creek that I wish to check out.

There are knots of grazing cattle around: cows with curly headed calves, fresh and white-faced; pregnant cows wide as pickups, hanging out with their best girlfriends; and the odd skittish heifer, all somewhat wild. They are scattered on the flats, along the timber edges and up into the trees on a small ridge to the east. I walk a half mile, enough of the wagon route to get the picture, and turn to commence the homeward trudge. After only a few hundred yards I hear a great bawling commotion from up on that ridge, and a cavalcade of a couple dozen perturbed cows on the semi-run comes streaming out of the timber and down the hillside toward me, tails high, udders swinging, scared by that long-distance bear I'd seen earlier, I imagine—the directions and distance are about right. A bear has a perfect right to try to make a living. I duck behind a small fir tree to circumvent an accident and watch and feel them pound by, drool flying, at close range. They turn and group themselves on some level open ground behind me.

The troop bellows a bit, then settles down to some serious digesting, but for one heifer that's still got her adrenalin up. She's already spied me and comes over on the dead run to investigate in that incredibly wall-eyed, young-cow way. She's never seen a walking human before, she hasn't had much life practice yet, and she's going to check me out and take me on if she feels it's necessary. She elects to take short, sharp, close-range runs at me each time I turn to walk away. I stare her in the eye, don't see too much happening there and realize I'm going to have to out-alpha this little gal or she just might run me over; she's got the edge on me in size and momentum. I hope I've got the edge in strategy. She's actually pawing the ground. We get down to a little system: me pre-thinking each of those runs of hers by wheeling around on her before she's got a good start, hurling a stream of my rudest insults and logger-type threats at her, fiercely brandishing my stick, and she backing up and trying again. Each run is a bit more reticent, and soon all I have to do is shake my stick at her; then a good, hard, directed stare, eye to eye, stops her for the moment. Finally she gives it all up as a lost cause, choosing instead to go stand close to a big, cud-chewing, lying-down, eyes-closed, black Angus mama who could care less whether I live or die.

> *The process of mythologizing is relentless, enduring and wild, and we are all part of it.*

I circle close to the creek and decide to cross at that shadowy willow and cottonwood thicket to see what those two ravens are up to. Tiptoeing across on a waterlogged windfall, I disturb the objecting ravens one more time and nearly step on the object of their rapt attention, a partially submerged black-and-white cow, bloated and half chewed and pecked, thick exposed leg joints glistening, hung up on the branchy end of the log I'm walking on. So that's what's been keeping that bear in the neighbourhood.

On my way back to the calving barn where I'm camped, I stop briefly at the little swamp on Koster Creek called, rather incongruously, Stinky Lake. There is still good late-afternoon light, and the valley is tinged in gold. I sit in my car with the door wide open, a can of Carling Extra Old Stock ("high test" as it used to be known) in one hand, and my 8 x 42 binocs in the other, watching birds: a pair of Wilson's warblers courting in the low willows, the male an intense yellow; coots random-gronking in open water; a mama goose hunkered on eggs on top of a muskrat house, head down, motionless, trying to look invisible, her partner resolutely patrolling the waters nearby. Yellow-rumped warblers chase each other from snag to snag. The season's first swallows, intent on the first bug-hatch, are swooping, diving and turning, and a cruising harrier passes casually through. There are mallards, shovellers, teal—all three kinds: green-winged, blue-winged and cinnamon—ring-necked ducks with heads bobbing, several invader starlings, flickers calling from waterlogged cottonwood snags, and territorial blackbirds flashing their bright red epaulets and loudly announcing their presence from last year's dead cattails.

I'M THINKING OF THE DAY'S EVENTS AND RECALL THE INCIDENT THAT OCCURRED that morning as I drove up the road out of Churn Creek on my way to Empire Valley and Grinder Creek. The road was slick, and I was paying full attention to staying on it, especially where the downhill side was a steep drop-off. I saw, or half saw, what I assumed was a stick about two or three feet long, lying crossways in a sunny patch on the road, and drove over or close to it. An intuition told me to look back at it in my rearview; I was startled to see that "stick" was vigorously thrashing, at times straight up and down, at the side of

Chilcotin horses on Clyde Mountain, Empire Valley. Photo courtesy of Chris Schreiber.

the road, a strange sight indeed. I quickly reversed for a better view and found that my "stick" had turned into a seemingly dead rubber boa snake, which in its last reflex had curled up into a rather tender-looking little coil, its head buried as if to hide, its tail up. That raised tail is a defensive posture meant to mimic the head. I had not seen a boa before, only heard and read about them; they are slab-sided, rubbery little creatures, and well named. These uncommon animals are at the cold edge of their range here and live mostly underground; they look subterranean. Their northern limits are roughly parallel to those of big sagebrush and some of the other semi-desert plants and animals up along here. I am not usually squeamish about such deathly matters, but I felt badly, as if somehow this was a death I could have avoided, that I had created an imbalance that needed righting, for nature, for myself.

Harry Marriott tells a good story about Phil Grinder in his last days. This story has to be a classic as both Lawrence Joiner at the O K Ranch and Mike Brundage in the Clinton Museum were quick to reel it off to me within a few minutes of my first meeting with each of them. It was the spring of 1914, and Marriott was riding by the Grinder ranch, down at the mouth of Big Bar Creek, on his way up to the Crows Bar range farther north. He had hoped to pay his respects, and spotting old Phil sitting outside his house in the warm spring sun, he stopped to say hello and talk. Stranger Wycott had just "gone over the high mountain" over at the Gang Ranch, where he had spent his last

Rubber boa snake, sometimes called the two-headed snake. Photo courtesy of Chris Harris.

years, and Harry mentioned his passing to the old man. Phil thought for a moment, turned slowly in his chair, shook his head, looked at Marriott and said, "Harry, ain't a man a damned fool to die in the spring of the year?"

Phil Grinder hung on until January 4 of the following year. He died shortly before his ninety-sixth birthday.

> *Did they sing all day*
> *Did they dance all night*
> *Did they ride their spade bit ponies*
> *Through the golden light*
> *Did they find true love*
> *Or was it all a bunch of lies*
> *Quin sabe, maybe it was paradise.*

—"Jaquima to Freno"
Ian Tyson and B. McIntyre

HERE AND NOW AT TWO CABIN LAKE

*Each moment has its own openness and intel-
ligence and precision, every moment, moment
after moment. If you can perceive that, to the
degree you can do that, you are really alive.*
—Peter Matthiessen, from a Tibetan teaching

I AM SITTING ON THE EDGE OF A STEEP ROCKY OUTCROP SOME 300 TO 400
feet above Churn Flats up Churn Creek. Immediately below me to the south
is Two Cabin Lake. This place where I happen to be is winter escape terrain
for California bighorn rams, it seems; the signs are all around. It is a mild,
early May day about high noon, and I am sitting, watching.

Three mule deer are picking their way along a centuries-old game trail
below me; one by one they enter into the narrow defile that separates this
cliffy hump from the high, timbered ridge to the east that I walked over this
morning. There is intention, clear, in their motion. After wintering in numbers on the low-elevation benches along the Fraser River, they are in slow
migration, following the snowmelt and spring green to higher country as far
southwest or west as the northern slopes of the South Chilcotin Mountains
and the Taseko Lakes seventy miles away. Though I am motionless, those
three pairs of big, brown, vigilant eyes have undoubtedly spotted me, and
the animals are walking purposefully and quickly to escape my line of sight.

I am sitting, watching, eating a slow lunch. There is nothing else to do right now. All is in its own time on and around this spiny little mount I am perched upon. When I sit, I sit; when I move, I move; when I'll leave, I'll leave. I breathe out, I breathe in; I pause and breathe out again. This, for this bright, extended moment, is the peace "which passeth all understanding."

ONE SPRING A YEAR OR TWO EARLIER, MY WALKING PALS, PETER STEIN AND Trevor Calkins, and I camped up Iron Gate Road at the edge of a meadow, not far from Hairy Fish Lake and, incidentally, right next to that five-mile Chinese ditch, dug in the 1880s for water to mine placer gold down on the Fraser. From a bend in the road north of there, we walked down to the open grassland at the bottom end of Churn Flats on a dog-leg route past Dry Lake. The lake was wet, temporarily, and inhabited by busy, happy ducks in a brief period of shrinking snowbanks, runoff and high groundwater.

Our aim was to walk as far west as we could comfortably go for a look up the flats and the country around. The day started warm; we walked for a couple of hours and from an open ridge above the flats got a good, long view up Churn Creek and to Wycott Flats beyond, across the creek, five more miles away. We could see the deep, shadowed breaks along the creek very well, and the dry, south-facing gulches edging the far side. That latter ground would be Gang Ranch land. On the south side of Churn and west of us, I could make out a steep, rocky point, behind where, from the map, I knew Two Cabin Lake would be. That name, "Two Cabin Lake," always gives me that old, slightly spooky feeling, like so many other place names up here: "Lone Cabin Creek," "Graveyard Valley," "Hungry Valley," "Little Paradise Creek." Two Cabin Lake has the ring of myth about it. I can just about hear the Ennio Morricone "spaghetti western" music, laden with that dramatic, Italian, on-the-money overstatement. The possibilities were enticing, but the day was

The possibilities were enticing, but the day was becoming hot. Mirages were beginning to shimmer and bend at the far end of the flats.

77

becoming hot. Mirages were beginning to shimmer and bend at the far end of the flats. It's no great pleasure to walk on seemingly endless grass flats in the heat, so we turned around and I was left to think and dream about the place.

The following winter I viewed a video from the Great Canadian Parks series on the Churn Creek Protected Area. In that piece there is a quick look at two log shacks by Two Cabin Lake, built by the McEwen brothers in the 1890s, or so the filmmakers state. My own estimate would be closer to 1908, the year the lots were pre-empted. The cabins, obviously long and thoroughly abandoned, were attractive against golden poplars and clean, bright blue, autumn sky. The thought of those sun-darkened old buildings up those flats somewhere gave me that familiar, deep-in-the-pit-of-my-gut, mystery feel and roused my all too readily activated curiosity and need to wander. I studied the 1:50,000 map of the area. I figured that, unlike our semi-circular, sun-scorched route that earlier spring, there must be an easier way to get there, some way to go straight northwest over what would be a forested ridge and come right down into that little basin and lake below the rocky point, simply by following a compass bearing. It was only three miles or so, depending on how much of it was drivable. The contour lines didn't look that steep. How difficult could it be?

When I returned the following spring to put my plan into motion, I found the route even easier than I had supposed.

RAIN FELL OVERNIGHT, SAVING ITS HEAVIEST FOR THE COOL OF EARLY MORN-ing as so often happens. The road gumbo is slicker than the previous day, and I drive slower than ten miles per hour to stay on the road. When I pass the spot where I drove over that boa snake the day before, I see it is gone; either it wasn't dead after all or, more likely, some fortunate scavenger was doing its job, reminding me that even we two-leggeds fit into the natural order of things. I fear the old track through the Riverside Forest Products property on the way up to my starting point might be a quagmire, but it's not, though a weather-worn, pickup-camper box sits at a startling angle off its green plastic milk-box props at the side of the road, and has obviously been that way all winter. Deer hunting happens in this protected area, and there are a few, mostly old, fall hunting campsites scattered through the timber. Up here, the country has that brown, seared look of late winter still; there is no fresh green. But the buds are fattening and the mutter of runoff water is everywhere. I park at the top end of a long, deep-rutted, gooey stretch, stow my lunch, dab on the day's Ombrelle sun-screen and move on out.

Over the hump, and a short way downhill on the other side at a spot where I have something of an overview, I take a compass reading, aiming at where, from the map, I estimate the aforementioned steep rocky outcrop should be. Then, compass in hand, I follow that bearing, 290 degrees west, down through the brush. After only a half-hour descent, I come out onto the top of a big gravel esker, exposed enough to see down into a pretty basin with a shallow grassland pond at the bottom, Two Cabin Lake. They call ponds and mud holes "lakes" here in big sage and bunchgrass country. The morning is windless and I see, even at that distance, the wake lines of active waterfowl across the water's mirror surface. There are a couple of good-sized poplar groves, oasis-like in the dry belt at this lowish elevation, at either end of the lake, and a somewhat wrinkled, pale, alkali flat along the far side; behind that is the steep-sided, talus-sloped rock outcrop. Looking west across Churn Flats and the Churn Creek breaks, I clearly see Wycott Flats extending far up-creek, and to the northwest the drainage system, once called China Creek and China Flats according to Harry Marriott, where old Stranger Wycott's long-empty homestead should be. I see, as well, the series of meadows and steep, bare slopes above and west of it that I will walk down to discover and see Wycott's place for myself.

I know the two cabins will be in or close to one or the other of the two poplar clumps; I choose the one to the west because it overlooks the flats, circle it, find nothing and start to cut across the alkali flat below the outcrop to check the other grove on the far side of the lake. The ground is covered with hoofprints, the wide, splayed marks of big animals cutting sharply through the crusted surface, and dotted with piles of sheep dung of a concomitant size, most of it fairly fresh. Clearly the rocky hump is an escape refuge for

Bighorn sheep escape terrain at Two Cabin Lake close to Churn Creek. The McEwens' barn is in the far poplar grove, and the remains of their cabin are on the exposed knoll to the right. Photo courtesy of Chris Schreiber.

mature bighorn rams: steep, south-facing, sufficiently large, with water and good feed in ready supply. While they have probably departed on their run to summer pastures already, they haven't been gone long, and I wonder if the ewes will be at lambing grounds up Churn Creek still, or if they have moved south also. I am curious, as well, about whether the salts of this pan provide some kind of mineral source for animals.

There is something else. At one end of the flats on a patch of bare rock, slightly elevated, is a set of stones arranged to make a seat. The view across the lake and up the wooded hillside is attractive, and I ask myself how many years and how long ago were people sitting at that place, enjoying the scenery, dreaming of home, making plans or wondering where the stock had moved to.

I continue on over to the second grove and find the buildings. The first, a little lean-to barn, its roof purlins still in place, is situated close to the lakeshore, behind a row of poplars. When it was first built, the lake would have

The McEwens' barn beside Two Cabin Lake, built about 1908. Photo courtesy of Chris Schreiber.

been just a few feet away; now the edge is another twenty feet farther out. Fresh reeds and sedges in between hide a peeping killdeer, mildly alarmed, and a couple of pairs of green-winged teal. The birds on this lake, a few mallards and goldeneye, a couple of coots, a lone grebe, eared or horned, seem edgy. There is a wide, marshy spring with open water behind the barn, and a wet, willowed draw continuing on uphill. The barn building is crude, as if it went up in a hurry, and was obviously made for short horses and short men, and probably not for the wild rose bushes that grow there now. The wall logs are shrunken, gnarled and gapped. Long manger poles were snugly notched into the walls at either end as the structure was being built. The door frames were hand drilled and dowelled to the log ends on either side in the usual manner for the times; nails were heavy and sparsely used then. A piece of curled boot leather protrudes from the earth floor.

I walk through poplars and rose bushes toward the cabin on a small open bench above the swamp, spotting a single dark chopped notch in a standing white trunk along the way; I expected more signs of old use. I see no indication of a corral at all. Poplar fence logs would go punky fast in these damp, densely brushed groves. The second building is roofless and much more dilapidated than the barn. The same method of dowelling was used in the door posts. I'm guessing the roof was sod and that it fell in from sheer weight. A single rhubarb leaf stands stark, vigorous and large already, inside, where a built-in pole bunk had been, in the moisture-retaining lee of the south-facing wall. A pale, desiccated version of that same plant survives in bleached earth outside, its original growing place against that same log wall.

A weathered horse skull gleams long-faced and white, even in the clouded light, against the ground near the door. There are old bones strewn all over this little basin, worn, short-shanked cow bones, numerous bighorn sheep bones, delicate deer scapula and hoofed leg bones, and dried coyote turds. Well-used game trails radiate out in all directions, including a couple of particularly dug-in grooves following the contours down off the hillside, like bent spokes on a wheel, all routes aimed at the water. The place has the look of a barnyard. This bench has been a watering and wintering area for animals for a long time: cattle in the old pre-"protected" days; a range of ungulates since the glaciers; cougars, naturally, on the prowl for hoofed meat, invisible, silent and close to their potential prey as usual; and now wolves and grizzlies are spreading back into the East Chilcotin—there is evidence of their existence all around. Winters must be tough for prey animals.

There is something raw and undeveloped about this place, as if it was never used much, except by animals. The buildings, while showing signs of skilled workmanship, seem simple, small and primitive, and worn mostly by weathering, as though they were never intended to be heavily used, except perhaps as a temporary cow camp, or to demonstrate "improvement" for pre-emption purposes. The two cabins look to be situated near the southern edge of lot 850 on the old, 1:250,000 National Topographic map series. According to Fred Knezevich, in a copy of his paper on the history of Empire Valley Ranch that I obtained from the Williams Lake Museum, in 1908 an Alexander McEwen pre-empted lot 840, covering a portion of the Churn Flats grasslands immediately southwest of 850. McEwen was likely in partnership with his older brother John at that time. Given the relatedness of those two lot numbers, and their obvious geographic and functional connection, I conclude that they were pre-empted simultaneously as an extension of the McEwens' earlier ranch properties farther south at Empire Valley. The location is choice: it is well-watered, south-facing and protected somewhat from winds, has good timber close by, and is handy to all that grazing country: the flats out front and downstream, and the open wooded slopes and grassy flats stretching southwest up Churn Creek. The area was probably used for summer range, as there are excellent wintering grounds up and down the low Fraser River benches closer to ranch headquarters. I have to believe it was a McEwen sitting there on that little stone seat of an evening a hundred years ago, surveying his domain and plotting the future. Was it he who planted the rhubarb? I note no lasting lilac bush by the cabin, no sign of settling in at all. There is little chance that a woman ever graced this modest oasis. Is that pipe tobacco smoke I smell?

Finding reliable information on the Empire Valley area, and especially on Empire Ranch itself, is like grabbing smoke, and relatively correct facts come reluctantly concerning the various McEwen brothers, who, it seems, were likely key to the consolidation of Empire Ranch properties in the 1890s. The little I do know about the McEwens is due mainly to Fred Knezevich, and to Don Logan's more recent researches, but even the apparent facts often seem contradictory and confusing. Packers used the Empire Valley area for wintering their stock likely as far back as the 1860s, but details as to who actually began the ranch and when are misty, particularly as various individuals made a range of pre-emptions in the area from the 1880s through to the start of the First World War.

It appears there was an earlier Alexander McEwen, born in 1840, who came out from Ontario, probably in the gold rush years (early 1860s), and who later worked as foreman for Thaddeus Harper, founder of the Gang Ranch. Exact dates regarding the Gang can be difficult to confirm given the vagueness of most opinions as to the actual year of its outset. Somewhere along the way, this original McEwen enlisted his grand-nephews John and

Sandy McEwen having his picture taken at Dog Creek, circa 1911. Annie Place, daughter of Joe and Jane Place of Dog Creek, is the photographer. Photo courtesy of Don Logan.

another, younger, Alexander McEwen, he of the 1908 Two Cabin Lake pre-emptions, born in 1874 and sometimes referred to as Sandy, to help him run what was becoming Empire Valley Ranch. The younger nephews eventually became owners of the ranch, but again we are not sure exactly when. An Alexander McEwen, the elder in all likelihood, initially claimed and later sold to Thaddeus Harper three lots (52, 53 and 54) close to the mouth of the Chilcotin River by McEwen Creek, perhaps so he might be free to develop the Empire Valley operation. The latter transaction was concluded in 1885. Incidentally, it was Alex McEwen the elder who found Thaddeus in 1884 lying unconscious, apparently thrown from and kicked by his horse. Though Mr. Harper survived, he had been significantly disabled by the accident.

Just to thicken the plot, Fred Knezevich introduces a fourth McEwen to his readers, a Thomas M., who, in my opinion (Don Logan concurs), is brother to the elder Alexander and inherited the ranch from him, but who quickly passed on ownership to his nephews, John and Sandy. There is a title notation, written with style, flourish and emphasis, in an early account book of the ranch, courtesy of the ever-vigilant history sleuth Don Logan. The account book, by its existence, establishes that as early as April 1, 1886, at least, the elder Alexander and Thomas McEwen were the operators and probable owners of the Empire Valley Ranch. The pride in that bold notation is hard to miss. Equally hard to miss is that date, 1886, which clinches the elder Alexander McEwen as primary founder of the Empire Valley Ranch. Sandy, born only twelve years earlier, was obviously too young for the job.

There were several other landowners in Empire Valley through those earlier years, including Calvin Boyle, who made his first claims early, possibly as far back as 1878, and Bryson and Carson, well-known ranchers from the Pavilion area and related to each other by marriage. The latter two men obtained land south of the present Empire Ranch headquarters to run sheep in the summer season. By the early 1890s, due no doubt to the advent of the reaction ferry across the Fraser River by the mouth of Churn Creek in 1890, homesteader settlement, including, among others, the Bishop brothers and the various members of the Brown family, father and sons, was increasing around and in Empire Valley. In 1890, Alexander McEwen added to his land holdings, pre-empting lot 154, the site of the present home ranch buildings, and adjacent lots 155 and 156 at the south end of Clyde Mountain. And in 1896, claims were made in Thomas's name for lots 363 and 364, on or close to lower Grinder Creek upstream from the ranch buildings. It may have been during this period that the original Alexander McEwen passed on. Then later, in 1908, as mentioned, the Two Cabin Lake lots over near Churn Creek were claimed by the younger McEwens. During that same decade, the brothers bought out the Boyle Ranch at the north end of the valley and the Bryson/Carson property south of Grinder Creek. But in 1910, after the flurry of all those land acquisitions over the years preceding, John and Sandy McEwen concluded their Empire Valley business by selling their outfit to John Kenworthy, an Englishman, and his wife. It seems the younger McEwens chose to sell out quite suddenly. Why do I suspect Mr. Kenworthy, with his English money, made them an offer they could not refuse?

Empire Valley Ranch headquarters. Photo courtesy of Marne St. Claire.

In 2000, the Churn Creek Protected Area was established, and the Two Cabin Lake basin is part of it. To allow for adequate winter habitat for bighorn sheep, particularly the regeneration of wild bunchgrass, cattle grazing along the flats has been restricted. The area is increasingly wild again, despite past pre-emptions, lot numbers, fences, cabins, old man-over-nature attitudes, a hundred-plus years of cattle ranching and that patchy, thirty- to forty-year-old, post-logging second growth on the hillside behind. No matter how hard the various McEwens, their crews and successors, and all the hunters there since shot away at the various "vermin" that frequented the area, or at mule deer for meat and bighorn sheep for their big horns, no matter to what extent they thought they owned it, the basin and area appear to have always been, in the last analysis, wild. It seems we have to live in a place for a while, last out a few winters, before we can begin to claim it and tame it, and even then such domesticity is predictably ephemeral, illusory and often short-lived. Great wild nature predominates.

I grew up influenced somewhat by those same earlier cultural assumptions and attitudes to wildlife—coyotes, wolves, hawks, gophers (ground squirrels), packrats, mice, rattlesnakes and bears, whatever wild critters were not confined to just two legs. Any wild beings that got in the way of our settler endeavours we attempted to eliminate, usually without much excess consideration. And to this day I'm not totally unsupportive of that old view, if the need is genuine and we are respectfully and fully conscious of our actions, and not endangering species. After all, we humans, settlers and city folks, are a part of the ecological equation. I trapped a rat in our attic a while back, killed him dead, and it wasn't a particularly elegant or silent death (though it was quick), but Ratty had to go; catch and release will not do, may his little rat soul rest in peace.

Up the North Thompson River at Darfield when I was little, and later at Port McNeill, a large, old-fashioned "family" logging camp then, on the north end of Vancouver Island, where I did much of my growing up, people shot at, trapped, netted, fished, caught, dug or otherwise removed and used wildlife. Hunting was central to our lives. Our neighbours at Darfield, the Schilling family, had chickens on their farm; so did we at our place. If a hawk flew over, the cry would go up, "A hawk, a hawk!" The chickens would be herded into their run and someone would go in to fetch the .22. If a coyote came trotting across a field, close and foolish enough to be in bullet range, it was shot at.

At Port McNeill it was the same. If somebody saw a wolf, he tried to shoot it. The North Island is not great deer habitat; too much of it is dense cedar swamp and salal brush, so often we had cougars in camp after dogs and cats, especially following a deep-snow winter. Blondie Arsenault would set deadfall traps, or the government cougar hunter from down-Island, a wiry, dark, tough-looking, legendary little man with a permanent five o'clock shadow, named Skate Haines, would be called to camp with his hounds to track the big cats down. No one questioned the necessity. Sometimes, as we sat there at our desks in rows in school, becoming ever so reluctantly civilized, we kids would hear the dogs on the chase, yelping and ki-yi-ing in the hills above camp, if the wind was right. Levi Wilson, two doors down from our house and right next to the school, shot a cougar sneaking down his raspberry rows as children played noisily on the school grounds in their lunch-hour break. That poor creature was young and ribby and desperate.

In those older times, we saw the timber in the valleys and on the hillsides, and the fish in the sea and rivers up and down the coast as accessible, exploitable and all but infinite; in a parallel way, we regarded wilderness and wild life as endless and forever.

Now we are learning that self-organizing, self-informing wilderness may be increasingly reduced across the land, but "wild" is everywhere, including in our own backyards, out on our downtown streets, and in and on our own bodies. A "wilderness," or what the great poet, bio-regionalist and essay writer Gary Snyder calls a "working landscape," is a wild place large enough and left sufficiently whole enough that it can sustain its own living integrity. And "wild" indicates a process that is largely beyond our control. Much of everything that is, including our own unconscious, personal and collective, our dream worlds and even some aspects of our behaviour, are beyond our ability to fully manage, especially as we are typically so ego-driven, and ego by itself is so notoriously short-sighted. Unexpected outcomes of our behaviours occur with frequency. In other words, much of everything that is, is wild. Words opposite in meaning to "wild" and "wildness," like "tame," "civilize," "domesticate," too often simply mean "inert," "lifeless," "dead."

In these times, the question necessarily becomes: do we aim to practise least harm, "Ahimsa," in our interactions with each other and all parts of the living world around us? And if so, what does that entail?

I RETRACE MY TRACKS BACK THROUGH THE POPLAR BOTTOM, ACROSS THE EDGE of the alkali flat, past all those ram prints and shit piles and bones, up the rumpled, rabbitbush-covered lower slopes toward the talus slides and crumbling red rock of the outcrop. Three-quarters of the way up the scree, under single large fir trees and at good south-facing lookout points, are multiple sheep beds,

My father, Pat Schreiber, hunting deer for the table near Darfield, BC, circa 1949. Photo courtesy of the Schreiber family.

smooth, sheep-sized, semi-level, dished-out places where the animals chew their cuds and watch. Clambering up on top, I find more prints and beds and a winter's worth of excreta; it's another barnyard up there.

According to the Churn Creek Protected Area Management Plan (2000), and biologist John Youds, California bighorn sheep along the Fraser River and lower Churn Creek are non-migratory; they reside near their winter ranges and move locally between seasonal habitats. But there are, or were, two separate herds of bighorn sheep up Churn Creek. One herd usually wintered around Churn Flats and Little Churn Creek, close to where I am right now, while the larger herd spent most of its winters around Wycott and Sheep Flats, up-creek, on the northern, sun-facing side of the valley. Each spring the herds migrated twenty-five to forty-five miles south to summer in the Red Mountain, Nine Mile Ridge, Yalakom Mountain areas, at or not far from the headwaters of the Yalakom River. Their migration patterns and

Bighorn sheep up Botanie Creek near Lytton. Photo courtesy of Marne St. Claire.

timing appear to have been quite separate and different from each other. It would be interesting to know how and why that might be.

I have prowled about that southern country to get a sense of some of that summer range for myself. On a warm August afternoon only a few years ago, Don Brooks and I spent an hour in the sun on the very top of Red Mountain, watching eleven relaxed ewes and lambs grazing and gamboling and moving about on an open slope below us. And just below them, on a warm point, a big mule deer doe lay chewing her cud, dozing and scanning the landscape in front of her for signs of potential trouble. She undoubtedly knew enough to use the presence of the ewes above and behind her to cover her back, but neither she nor the sheep seemed aware of us up there on the mountain in the sky above them.

I was talking with Chilco Choate over at Gaspard Lake about wildlife matters some time back. He hunted or guided hunters on the north side of Churn Creek for decades and, after fifty years of year-round wilderness watching throughout the area, and having an inquiring intelligence, has learned much about animals. He remarked that the wildlife biologists think sheep winter in the same place every year, but his own observations over a much longer period have informed him that this is not necessarily true.

I asked him simply, but loudly, "Why not?" Choate is quite deaf, probably because of all those high-power rifle cartridges exploding next to his ear; I'm guessing his right ear is worse than his left.

He paused. "Food supply," he said, and after further thought, "Disturbance."

TO BEGIN TO KNOW WILD LIFE IN ITS COLLECTIVE COMPLEXITY AND intelligence at all, we need to be out there watching and absorbing long-term, for parts of as many seasons of the year as possible. We need to observe some of the same settings over and over to spot the differences, the changes, the anomalies, the various interactions. I am a dilettante in such matters, but I have learned that it is good and useful sometimes to be out there in the wild in silence and alone. When we are by ourselves in wild places, we naturally maintain our alertness; we become a part of the silence and stillness around us. To be able to observe wild animals, their sign, and the ways that lives interconnect in wild nature is a profound privilege and practice; empathy is at the core of such practice, I believe.

Smaller numbers of California bighorn sheep are scattered farther west around the outlying mountains adjacent to Taseko Lake and Nemaiah Valley, to the southwest around the headwaters of Big Creek, and elsewhere along the wilder, dryer edges of the South Chilcotin Mountains. During an August snowfall in 1993, on a high, alpine ridge above Lorna Lake, the primary source of Big Creek, Don Brooks and I followed the ghostly pale bobbing rear ends of two or three bighorns ahead and below us, just barely visible in a sky of fat snowflakes. They and we were noiseless in fresh snow. We all dropped down to Elbow Pass, where the precipitation was turning to rain. The sheep carried on over the divide into upper Tyax Creek. Don and I split off to follow a swollen, boot-soaking creek down into Graveyard Valley to look for the gravesite near where Graveyard and Little Graveyard Creeks come together. It was there, later that afternoon, that we met Barry Menhinick, father to Warren, riding alone on a pinto horse. That was our first of a series of memorable times in his company (including a ten-day round-the-Chilcotin Mountains horse-trip with him a year or two later); we stopped not far from the old grave mounds sinking into earth to bullshit for most of an hour in the pelting rain.

Another time back in the '80s, high up on a rocky shoulder on Taseko Mountain above Taseko Lake, Don and I had a group of seven sheep, mainly ewes, watch us carefully one morning as we cooked and ate breakfast below them. Like Mount Ts'yl-os (named Tatlow by early mapmakers once upon a time) above Nemaiah Valley, Taseko Mountain stands like a sentinel, almost alone. Both mountains stand well over ten thousand feet, within one foot of being the same height as each other actually, and are similarly massive and imposing. Bighorn sheep seem to be able to live and survive at high elevations on Taseko's exposed and windswept south-facing flanks, maybe especially around that steep-sloped hump and saddle where we were camped above the lake. We were warned of the sheep's presence by the sound of falling rock behind us. We turned and looked up to see seven bighorn profiles outlined against the skyline, quite close above us, resting and chewing cud. At any instant, at least one sheep would be faced to us, intent, head motionless (but for those sideways-grinding jaws) and eyes fixed, watching all our moves for danger signs. It's disconcerting to be stared at so pointedly when you're attempting to cook a gourmet meal in wilderness.

Migration into backcountry has to be a risky business for California bighorns. Sheep prefer open country and count on escape terrain close by. They depend for their safety on their excellent eyesight, agility and speed, and their collective vigilance on the exposed sloped rock, open grasslands and sub-alpine terrain they prefer. To shift habitats from winter to summer to winter again, as did the two migratory herds in their annual travels from Churn Creek to Red Mountain and as far south as Yalakom Mountain and back, they must move down into less-familiar wooded territory with limited escape terrain. Those would be long and vulnerable miles to be so exposed to possible predation. I've heard it said that, typically, when sheep migrate they move quickly. My brother, Chris, was driving along the Jesmond road east of the Fraser in the month of May, years back, when he spied a good-sized band of bighorns crossing the road in front of him at a fast trot, headed eastward for the nearby Marble Mountains it looked like.

There is even a tiny, slightly apocryphal sheep herd far to the northwest in the westernmost windblown extremities of the Ulgachuz Mountains above Anahim Lake in caribou land. Those would be, by far, the northernmost California bighorn sheep on the continent. They may be last remnants from a warmer, drier grassland era that peaked about five thousand years ago.

Local stories from around Anahim have it that some clown, no doubt anxious to kill something, shot the only mature bighorn ram in that little sheep group. In time, Fish and Wildlife helicoptered in replacement studs, probably from that great, dry-belt, California bighorn source, the Junction herd. Meanwhile, so the story goes, the miscreant, a local, was sought out by a few of the Anahim Lake folks, imbued, no doubt, with a strong need for ecological equilibrium, and given a thorough pummeling for his dubious judgment. Once again, natural balance was restored to the region.

I reach the very top point of the escape mount and take the time to look around me across to that broken series of dry gullies, ridges and gulches on the north side of Churn, then to the west and southwest up the creek, and east over to Gang Ranch. I can see their freshly ploughed hayfields, tiny in the far distance, dark brown against the pale spring green and tan of big sagebrush and old grass. At a grasslands conference in Williams Lake in 2001, I heard forestry researcher Ray Coupe say that there may be a few pon-derosa pines across Churn Creek on the south-facing dry side, which, if true, would be unusual. Those ponderosas ("yellow pine" to many rural folks), if they have survived the ravages of the pine bark beetle, would be among the most northerly on the continent. He said also that someone had seen whitebark pine there, well below its normal sub-alpine elevation, courtesy of cone-stashing Clark's nutcrackers, and these two pine species, together with ubiquitous lodgepole pines, would make that place a rarity for the dry Interior: three species of pine trees growing in the same setting.

Below me on the south side is Two Cabin Lake, flat and calm. The day is a little cool, but perfect. I decide to stay up there and eat lunch, absorb the silence and just sit. My inclination is to "keep my nose open and my eye on the skyline" as the old-time mountain men used to say back in the old, dangerous, mythy days. That coiled boa on the road edge continues to lurk in a corner of my mind. I swallow a few mouthfuls of water, eat my sandwich, watch those passing mule deer below me, drink a bit more water, say a small "thank you" to whatever it all is, sniff the air a little for intruders and, quiet and alone, just sit there. The wild and silence and liveliness of this place and my own quiet, incur a slow surrender. When I sit and watch, I sit and watch...

As I sit, I am struck by the subtle symmetry of the place: the basin and lake, a gentle rounded depression, an otherwise empty space holding water, and this rocky escape mount I'm on where wild rams find refuge, a humpy protrusion up, out, onto the grass flats—two profiles in balance, one negative, one positive, one down, the other up, all of it open to the sunny southwest.

Time alone in a wild place is time in the present tense, particularly if we've been out there for a while and are paying attention. Occasionally, when I'm alone in the bush or up on some high silent place, I stop and turn to look around and, in an unhurried manner, fix my attention on each of the four directions, the four cardinal points of the compass, east to north, one by one. I take time, as well, to cast my vision down to the rock and earth beneath my feet, and up that same axis to the infinite light sky.

Time alone in a wild place is time in the present tense, particularly if we've been out there for a while and are paying attention.

This is a way to more thoroughly know, in this moment, where I am, where I have come from, where I may be going and what my place might be in it all. It is a gesture of acknowledgment and respect and conscious connection to the subtle, powerfully wild, great world around us. It feels like a form of prayer. Such orientation is primal.

The words of writer, traveller, naturalist and Zen teacher Peter Matthiessen, one of the great defenders of our natural world, quietly resonate: *This present moment, extraordinary; each moment, extraordinary.* I take a slow breath and give thanks one more time. These years, I find myself saying thank you often, wherever I am; given the richness of this world and my own place in it, my need to do so is continually self-evident.

After a while, when the moment seems right, I leave, angling down the talus carefully, using my walking stick to prevent a tumble. That third leg on the downhill side is handy as you approach full maturity. I follow one of those game ruts above that willowed draw, up to where it braids out below the top of the ridge. More walking through dark, uphill fir woods brings me to a barbed-wire fence below the old track. I clamber over, stepping up the strands of wire tight against a post delicately, without altering my person all that much.

I reach my vehicle and drive down the mud road a short distance to turn at a branch track aimed west to see if I can look down into Little Churn Creek. Immediately I come to a small, human-made clearing with, at one side, a massive, double-wide trailer with a heavy tow hitch, properly levelled and supported, well worn in, with the requisite porch, woodpiles, biffys, stove-oil and gas barrels, and considerable yard junk, including large numbers of deer hooves, some neatly laid out in rows, and the odd leg bone, well gnawed.

The back door is open and I walk inside. The place is well appointed, with a skookum cookhouse-type stove and a neatly welded water-heater on top, cupboards, some mostly non-perishable food supplies, small scatterings of mouse poops, a long table, chairs, posted breakfast and dinner menus, pictures on the walls, hunting magazines on a bench, a couple of empty booze bottles on a shelf and a well-used journal hanging on a nail. Everything is covered in dust. There is a mini, cedar-lined sauna off one wall. A bunk room for eight takes up the final third of the building. The place is a regular Best Western.

I study some of the pictures: group photos of big, cheerful, hairy guys with beers (not unlike myself, except they are all in camouflage outfits). They appear to be led by a man named Wolfgang. There is something about his presence. I'll bet he is the fine welder; he looks like a well-trained, fine-detail sort of man. There are shots of camouflage guys with three days' growth and that fulfilled "got my breath back, time for a smoke" expression, kneeling on the shoulders of glassy-eyed mulies looking as if something hard just hit them; shots of smiling sweeties with large rifles held gingerly; obviously a decent, good-natured group overall, "salt of the earth" folks, bonhomie to spare, but what was this backcountry mecca, as big as a bowling alley, doing here? I thought this was a park, or at least a protected area, a place of refuge for beleaguered four-leggeds, sometimes, to rut and winter.

I read parts of the journal. It has entries from all over—Langley, New Westminster, Port Alberni, "The Lake" (Williams Lake), Prince George and smaller, lesser places—and a range of testimonies about the greatest times ever, comments about dead deer, deer missed, deer that should have been dead but weren't, snow, fun, hangovers, kids getting lost, snowmobiles, broken-down snowmobiles, more fun, more snow, storms, cougars, bighorn sheep...Now hold it. I easily understand that, with the large numbers of mule deer continuing to winter at lower elevations along the west side of the Fraser River, a few less reinforce the wily and help conserve habitat, but bighorn sheep? I thought the function of Churn Creek Protected Area was to regenerate blue-bunch wheatgrass and help preserve California bighorns, of which, estimates indicate, there are fewer than 3700 in the entire province. There may well be fewer than that, given the radical effects of past lungworm epidemics and the consequent pneumonia, plus predation and human encroachment on some wild sheep ranges. A further purpose of the CCPA was to demonstrate that game and good range management, and a functioning, well-managed cattle ranch (Empire Valley Ranch) can co-exist side by side, a fascinating, creative and utterly worthy experiment. But I feel a bit confounded by these seeming contradictions and wonder if a cash-strapped Parks Ministry is capable of adequately managing the place.

It's possible that in the CCPA some deer-hunting camps are too close, some roads and tracks too handy, to bighorn sheep winter range up along Churn Creek and elsewhere. Consider bush travel by ATV: if I can walk it, some guy can ride it, at thrice the speed. I grew up hunting in a hunting world; I know too well that, although the large majority is, not all hunters are ethical. Some are thoughtless and greedy, and a few just like to kill. Disturbance is disturbance, and it takes only one or two to do damage.

Calving barn at the entrance to Empire Valley. Photo courtesy of Chris Schreiber.

Earlier, setting up camp at the calving barn down at Empire Valley, I was already getting the impression that management might be less than optimal, although, to be fair, it was early in the spring season. The privy was filthy, there was garbage around, the main gate was falling off its post and, worst of all, campers had been burning fires inside the obviously flammable, creosote-timbered building, using corral rails and posts for fuel; the place was at risk, and signs needed to be posted for the benefit of the thoughtless.

Days later, when I get back to Williams Lake, I attempt, with kind assistance from my good friend Sage Birchwater, to make some contacts regarding my concerns. I find a new version of an old story; our new provincial government is making changes, for its own sake, I would say, or for the sake of egos and ideology. How many times over the decades, no matter what political stripe, have I seen this? Employees are being laid off and ministries are being changed, shuffled and renamed; employees appear bewildered and unable to tell me who works for which, and where. I find confusion, fatalism and few sentient bodies. An old contact in the Parks Ministry has retired, rather prematurely I think, and it seems as if there is nobody left to get out of the office to observe, learn and do something. I read in the newspapers later that year that two BC provincial parks, Manning and Strathcona, both large and heavily used, have one, count them, one, full-time employee each, plus seasonal part-timers we presume, to carry on with management and maintenance. I also learn, first-hand, that Wells Gray is another similarly impoverished park, and I'm sure there are many more. Wherever I go, I hear there are nowhere near enough park and game wardens (conservation officers) to adequately do their wildlife assessment and management jobs around the province. Who has the time, practice and personal authority to truly speak for wild places?

I hear (and observe) that local bighorn sheep populations have been decreasing in the last several years—significantly, it turns out. My recent contacts with some helpful Fish and Wildlife personnel confirm that. Generally, herd numbers are much lower now than at their population peaks in 1995. Most herds are stabilized, but the combined numbers of those two migratory herds based up Churn Creek continue to plummet to a probable total, so far, of fewer than forty animals. This depression is so severe that the Wildlife Branch has shut down hunting in the Fraser–Churn Creek area. I'm not surprised to hear this. As serious as the lungworm-pneumonia issue has been in the past, a major cause now, west of the Fraser River, appears to be predation. Wolves spreading east across the Chilcotin Plateau have become a problem for ranchers and an increased threat to wild ungulate herds along the Fraser River. Bighorn sheep and great numbers of mule deer winter on the lower, warmer, benches where there is lighter snowfall. Several times while driving north up the west side of the Fraser to Big Bar ferry in late April or early May I've seen deer in herds of three to forty, adding up to many hundreds. In my spring wanderings around Blackwater Lake and the Goose Lakes, and down to and around Wycott's place across from Two Cabin Lake, the signs (stripped deer bones, hides and hooves) of fresh wolf kills are everywhere. A large deer population must attract carnivores to some bighorn sheep winter ranges, which in my opinion are situated close to wintering deer pastures in certain places.

ON MY MOST RECENT VISIT TO EMPIRE VALLEY IN THE SPRING OF 2013, I AM happy to see improvements at the calving barn since my walk down into the Two Cabin Lake basin those years back. New corrals have been built, fences and gates mended, the roof patched, the water source improved and the open front of the building closed off to vehicles. Most importantly, fires have been banned anywhere near the highly flammable building. There seems to be an increase in managerial attention given to this invaluable place; and I've finally signed up as a Friend of Churn Creek Protected Area.

A Say's phoebe greets me when I first walk into the dark of the barn. These lovely members of the flycatcher family are uncommon in the Chilcotin, but I've been observing Say's phoebes there, including nesting females, since my first visit to the place in 2001. I am grateful for their persistence and liveliness.

THE JUNCTION

...here there is no place that does not see you.
You must change your life.
— Rainer Maria Rilke

HOW DO YOU TALK ABOUT THE JUNCTION?

Not easily, it seems. So let us begin by stating that the Junction is, most obviously, a pair of deep crevices in the surface of the Cariboo-Chilcotin plateau. These crevices merge into one where two great rivers—the Fraser from out of the north and its tributary, the smaller Chilcotin (Tsilhqot'in), from out of the northwest and southwest—come together. The Junction is, as well, the land between and around the rivers, humped and rolling and largely unwooded, rock, clay, grassland, big sage, and deep breaks and gullies along the margins. The Chilcotin side, particularly steep in some places and, facing southwest, is the more sun-baked and open. Those two rivers—the former, mud-brown when you're up close; the latter, blue-green and opaque with glacial rock-flour—flow 2000 to 2500 vertical feet below the height of land between them. But for those quicksilver rivers at the bottom, this land is virtually waterless. At times it is breathlessly hot.

Once, many years ago in the spring, about the time I came into the Chilcotin country for the first time, I visited the north side of the Grand Canyon of the Colorado River in the United States. I tried to grasp the immensity of

The Chilcotin River at Farwell Canyon near Riske Creek, showing the steep clay cliffs and hoodoos characteristic of the Junction area. Photo courtesy of Marne St. Claire.

the place. I tried but I never could quite comprehend it. Each morning and evening, over two or three days, I dutifully walked to the edge, near where we were camped on the north side, to get the measure of it. I could note its vastness and depth, and its shifting beauty in the late spring light, but, being huge, wild and ancient beyond eons, the Grand Canyon overwhelmed me, though my memories of it are indelible.

In a similar way here in Central British Columbia, the Junction, though not nearly so vast or so deep, has seemed sometimes to be beyond my capacity to fully comprehend and acknowledge. The beauty of the canyons, the grassland slopes, the contours of the land, the rivers below, fascinates me, but I find the power of the place unnerving a little. There is nowhere like it, that I know of, in this province.

A trip down into the Junction is simple enough if it hasn't rained too hard or long. The route is steep in places and potentially slick, but the scale of it is not huge: a few miles of walking, at most, if we drive the first several slow, up-and-down miles in. However, having thought and talked about it, and walked parts of the lower southern end, I come away with a deepening impression that, as long as mountains stand and those two great rivers flow, the Junction remains, in essence, a constant, impermeable and unchanging.

Paradoxically, it appears sometimes that the Junction is not actually there. Gazing across at it, peering down into it, imagining walking or driving it, can feel a bit like clutching at air. The place recedes as I view it; it fades past the edges of my vision and knowledge of it. It becomes a place with no sound, no smell, no taste; you cannot touch it. It seems beyond reach. But on either side of me below, the two rivers bend and turn and flow on, inexorably, in and out of sight.

Sometimes the Junction seems dimensionless. In looking at it, in being by it or in it, despite its 2500 feet of elevation from bottom to top, it appears to have no depth. All is backdrop or foreground. The sense of distance is lost. The rolling hills and snow-topped mountains, which logic, habit and maps tell us are away in the distance, are immediately in front of us or not there at all. Three-dimensional perspective is missing, misplaced, put aside, forgotten in haze, smoke, dust, in passing thunder clouds, lightning flashes, quick rain. And still the conjoined rivers flow away in that strange, seemingly motionless way rivers of power have when viewed from a high distance. Is it the relentlessness of their combined flow south that seems to drain the place of its temporal substance?

There are places of unusual power and attraction across this land. Like most fellow walkers and travellers, I have experienced such places from time to time: a tall mountain standing alone, a basalt-columned hump, a certain rich lake or swamp, a particularly high or lively waterfall, a hidden valley, caves, ancient camping places where people lived their lives out long, long ago. The Junction may be such a place, a place with some myth-significance perhaps, where time becomes timeless and we slip more easily into a kind of myth-mindedness. Myth-mind is another way of seeing, one that allows us to experience and know more thoroughly the range of possibilities in this world. That range is wider than we imagine. This is a wild and watchful and reciprocal world we walk through.

Life at the Junction carries on. Most of it is protected range for California bighorn mountain sheep under the joint auspices of the provincial Ministry of Parks and the Riske Creek Ranching Company, the latter based at what was, once upon a time, the old Becher place at Riske Creek. Much of the land north of the sheep range is owned by the ranch, and much of the rest by the adjacent Toosey First Nation. Cattle-grazing densities are managed, and the return of bluebunch wheatgrass, and the surrounding ground lichens that fix nitrogen and preserve moisture, is encouraged. Bunchgrass is more nutritious by far than domestic grass species and is fundamental to bighorn sheep survival in long, cold winters. In the past, the Junction range has been home to one of the largest concentrations of California bighorns in North America, if you include sheep in nearby ranges down the Fraser River and along the grassy benches and escape breaks west up Churn Creek.

But since the late 1990s, wild sheep populations in the Junction, Fraser River and Churn Creek ranges and elsewhere in parts of southern BC have been radically reduced. For some time now, in most old sighting spots around Farwell Canyon on the lower Chilcotin River, and down the Fraser River, I'm not seeing bighorns as often. It is worth noting that hunting has been closed in the Junction since 1998.

My sightings around Farwell, fairly frequent in earlier decades, were almost always of groups of females and lambs. Junction ewes and their offspring apparently live mainly on the west side of the Junction, lambing in the steep ravines above the river, I expect. In recent years, the only sheep I saw down there were two ewes in seeming distress by the Farwell Bridge. I was standing stock-still, waist deep in sagebrush, and one of them, calling constantly and plaintively as if she had lost something, her lamb maybe, or her herd mates, trotted in my direction and all but bumped into me. I assume she had seen me but was distracted.

Often wild animals do not become unduly alarmed if you remain motionless. I had a Rocky Mountain ewe near Banff one time come up on the dead run as I stood there and proceed to use my hand vigorously and noisily as a salt lick, an unaccustomed and odd experience for me, but apparently not for her. Sheep have warm, rough, sloppy-wet tongues, if I'm to generalize from this sample of one.

So, bighorn sheep are a major part of and reason for the preservation of the Junction, its ecological integrity and diversity, its presence, its being.

Cattle range just north of the Junction Sheep Range Provincial Park. Photo courtesy of John Schreiber.

For sure, they are a central part of the attraction. We venture down there in hopes always of spotting them in the sage or out on some lookout point, of noting their vigilance and watching them walk, of learning their habits and gaining further glimpses into their inscrutably wild sheep ways. We might admit they are the signature "totem" animal for that place as salmon, for example, are for the Fraser River drainage in general and, come to think of it, as packrats must surely be for the calving barn over at Empire Valley.

The first time I drove down to the bottom end of the Junction, I saw a small herd of Californias, young males I believe. I'd been driving up and down the Farwell Canyon road for years, always casting a wistful eye at that nondescript little dirt turnoff at the top of the hairpin corners, curling off south into the unknown, the access route to another of those Chilcotin-type mystery places. One day I decided to follow it: the migrating birds were crazy with spring; I had half a tank of gas and lunch makings, including a can or two of Okanagan Springs IPA in the cooler; there was a wide north-south strip of clear blue sky, a "Fraser River trough," overhead, so why not? Never mind that a dark weather front was moving in from the west.

It was mid-May. The nip of early spring was still in the air, and dandelions were greening and beginning to bloom in sunny, damp places. As I drove, the sky was turning to a steely shade of grey. A concern about getting caught in a deluge lurked in a corner of my mind. Chilco Choate had just told me about the sheep researchers, years back, who were marooned for days after a hard rain on the bottom end of those steep, rolling, clay gumbo slopes that characterize the Junction road. Clay-dirt is deceptive: a nice easy dusty slow drive one day; deep greasy ruts the next. This is four-wheel-drive country. So there was a slight edge to this side trip and I was in a bit of a hurry.

I got to the overlook above the bottom end of the Junction comfortably enough, but the track down through parkland poplar groves out onto rolling grassland slopes, with a few Hereford whitefaces grazing and looking relaxed after winter, was a slow and winding thing. There were steep, dry, "four-wheel high" hills to crawl down or up, but nothing to strain the Pathfinder. I passed two or three small, dry marshes on the way down, none appearing to have held water for months, or years more likely. Groundwater levels are dropping in these warming, changing times. I drove tentatively over a decrepit, mildly dangerous-looking, wooden cattle guard, passed by the semi-trashed research cabins in a clump of trees farther south and reached the final, bare, steep-sided lookout point and the two deep canyons closing in on either side below me. I could see far in three directions under a heavy sky. The rivers, where they were visible to the south, looked like moving lava. A newish snake rail fence cut off wheeled access to the grassy flats and steep cliffs and breaks below. If I wanted to get down to the fabled meeting point of the Fraser and the Chilcotin, two-plus steep miles farther on, I would have to get out and walk.

Close by stood a handsome stone monument to Choate's good friend Harold Mitchell, a wildlife biologist and the man most responsible for the existence of this sheep range. He died down south at Shulaps Mountain in the Yalakom River area in a helicopter crash in 1981. *Shulaps* means "bighorn ram" in the language of the Lillooet (St'at'imc) people down there; *yalakom* means "bighorn ewe." This linguistic distinction likely indicates the separate summer grazing areas of the ram and ewe herds.

California bighorn sheep in the Junction. Photo courtesy of Chris Harris, author of *Spirit in the Grass.*

That point between the two rivers has always been a kind of magic place for me. I first laid eyes on the Junction a long time ago, on my occasional summertime comings and goings up and down the Dog Creek road to the south. There is a place at a tight bend in the road above Little Dog Creek that faces up the river benchlands north and looks right at the Junction and the canyon of the Chilcotin veering in from the northwest. The first time I saw that view from there, the air was blue and thick with smoke. This served to accentuate a misty, faraway, two-dimensional sense of the place; those pale, sun-burned slopes and ravines looked as if they had been etched. The Junction had presence, a kind of ethereal massiveness, even from four miles away. I knew I had to go and walk around there some day.

At that spot, just before the road curls down into the creek gully, a small cluster of old ranch buildings had stood, and bits of ranch junk lay scattered about. Later the buildings were burned out, whether by accident or design I do not know. I miss them. They added a layer of timeworn human liveliness to the picture. The ranch headquarters had clearly been located at that particular place for that soul-soaring northern view.

The ranch was established soon after the gold rush by Magnus Meason, a well-educated Englishman, fluent in Latin and Ancient Greek apparently, who, with his aboriginal wife, raised a good family there. He was a man of substance, so they say; Little Dog Creek on some old maps is named Meason. Across a grassy slope, facing in that same northerly direction, is a white picket fence enclosure with a sizable gravestone in it. I walked over there one day to examine it and read the inscriptions. It seems Mr. Meason lived a long life. It seems also that he was accompanied to the afterworld by two of his adult children if the other names and dates on the stone are any clue. It was as if the graves were placed out there to give whatever souls inhabited the place a running jump into eternity, or wherever souls go, in the manner of many old Indian grave sites placed in high places across the province. Old fence boards lay around; the standing ones were brightly white. I saw no mention of Mrs. Meason. She may be buried at Alkali Lake.

Some of the first gold findings on the mid-Fraser River were at or near the Junction. Peter Dunlevy and his companions, who were later to make a rich strike in the Horsefly area, placer-mined on the west bank just below the Junction in 1859. Grant Keddie, of what is now the Royal BC Museum in Victoria, did extensive archaeological work around the Junction and kindly drew me a rough map of the location of pithouse sites near the point of meeting of the two rivers. He said they were below a steep hillside in some poplar trees on the east side. Sage Birchwater had been to the flats on the opposite side of the mouth of the Chilcotin, down

The gravesite of members of the Meason family near Little Dog Creek. Photo courtesy of Marne St. Claire.

off a Gang Ranch road, and had seen kekuli holes over there also. We talked of seeing signs there of the workings of the Chinese placer miners in the wake of the Cariboo rush: rows and rows of sorted rock piles on a long, miner-made bench, and the remains of shelters, particularly one, a large, rectangular, log-reinforced room dug into the clay bank above the river. I note that the three major rapids on the lower Chilcotin are named Chinaman Flat, and Railroad and Caboose Rapids. In 1883, Thaddeus Harper of the Gang Ranch bought the piece of land (lot 47) that encompasses the small flat on the point where the two great rivers meet as part of a two-river crossing and holding place there for his cattle herds. That was before the Churn Creek Ferry and the Gang Ranch Bridge were established downriver in 1890 and 1914 respectively.

So I was standing behind the log fence, scanning, trying to glass signs of the past at the bottom of the Junction across two miles of sagebrush, clay slopes and cliff edges, when I noticed or felt movement to one side of me through the fence rails. I stepped up to look over and there, slightly below me, about forty feet away in a tight clump, were eight or nine nervous, young, thickset bighorn rams, smallish horns, no lambs, jumpy, trying to decide what to do. I flinched or twitched, I stared too hard, or the beat of my heart was audible and off they went. They ran as a single tight unit, their churning, off-white rear ends signalling they were gone, curling down and away over the steep, grassed, rolling slope to the closest gullies on the east side. They disappeared in what seemed like an instant, and I was left with a quick picture in my mind of their meaty ham muscles driving, hyper-powered, over the edge and out of sight. It felt a little strange in those moments to be looking down at them.

One warm afternoon that same year, in Empire Valley by Brown Lake, Marne and I met Ed Prior from Miocene driving by in a matter-of-fact manner in his homemade, well-crafted, half-sized covered wagon, freshly and brightly painted, and pulled by an obliging team of horses. We were startled momentarily by this miniature, out-of-time "wagon train" vision from the past. Ed was just returning from a circular tour of that lonely benchland country down south towards Lone Cabin Creek. In talking with him, we discovered that he once had had a job counting and studying bighorn sheep in the Junction area. Among other things, he had learned that bighorn ewes and rams move in separate herds for most of the year, and he confirmed that rams inhabit the more wooded east side of the Junction along the Fraser; the ewes range along the west side. The ewes with their lambs move more slowly and covertly, having different survival needs. Those sheep at the Junction that I spooked not only had somewhat longer, thicker horns and chunkier bodies than bighorn ewes, but they were also racing for escape terrain on the east side; for sure they were young rams.

The dark season's snowbanks lie slowly melting in the damp dark spruce woods. I'm descending out of winter into spring again.

There is not a lot to say about my second venture down into the Junction. It was July of 2003, the summer of no rain, extreme heat, and smoke in the air just about everywhere. There were serious forest fires in British Columbia's dry-belt country, the land of over-age lodgepole pines like standing fire bombs, mostly free of fires for a hundred years, and waiting to release their pent-up combustibility. I wanted to show Marne this intriguing place, so down we went. It was hot high noon and the country was bleached the colour of straw. One of my rear tires picked up something sharp, probably at that dilapidated cattle guard, and we found ourselves on a steep, dusty hillside, not far from the university research cabins, with a slow tire-leak and no flat place to fix it. This was not good.

The jacks on Japanese cars, finely engineered though they may be, are designed for level asphalt in a more orderly, flat and level world, with no margin for variations like deep mud, rutted sidehills or even a little loose gravel. The set of track ruts we found to work on faced south. The heat was intense, mind bending, and I was beginning to not think, to panic slightly. It was as if there was some large being up there in helmet, goggles and oily coveralls with a welding torch and an attitude; my eyeballs were going gritty from the piercing sunlight. I had not had my light-distorting cataracts removed yet. Marne saved the moment by passing me the water jug and holding up a tarp to cut off the sun's glare so I could see what I was doing. I changed the tire with few delays and only minimal destruction, and we got out of there. We had no zeal to challenge the sun gods any further on that particularly moistureless, joyless afternoon. Our visit to the Junction had felt like a small-scale descent into the steaming cauldrons of heck.

Cold drinks later under the poplars at Sage Birchwater's place overlooking Williams Lake were a boon, a balm and a refuge, gratefully accepted. Let's hear it for refrigerators, ice-cube trays and some of the other trappings of the modern world! Don't ice cubes in sunlight, and a slice of yellow lemon, look and sound wonderful, glinting and tinkling in a glass? That light positively dances.

The following day I marched out and bought a whole new set of four-plies. You can't just buy a single tire when you've blown one on a four-by-four; the real four-wheel-drive world does not work that way.

So, it is one year later, May 2004, and early in the season. The day is bright and cool. There is a light edge to the westerly wind and the air is clear. I can see the Marble Mountains, capped with snow, far to the southeast, though they look a mere five miles away. I have left the Gang Ranch cow camp at Gaspard Lake, and Chilco Choate at his place a short mile to the west; the first migrating killdeers and Canada geese are sounding their presence; and the dark season's snowbanks lie slowly melting in the damp dark spruce woods. I'm descending out of winter into spring again. I'm headed to the bottom of the Junction. I have time, gas, water, and I'm travelling alone. Driving or walking by myself gives me silence, a certain freedom and the maximum opportunity to be where I am, to hear and feel the place I am in, to try to plumb the layers of what is and my place in it in this country. No better place or time to be than now at the Junction.

I have been alone for several days. I've driven up the West Fraser road, crawled down to Watson Bar, looked down that famous Big Bar Ferry hill, and upriver to Crows Bar and the mouth of Lone Cabin Creek; I will get up (or down) to more of those wild river places sometime. I could just about see Empire Valley at the far end of that long view. I drove all around Big Bar Mountain on an evening with Lawrence Joiner, spotting old homestead sites in the gloom. I've looked down on the Fraser River and across to China Gulch from the front side of Clyde Mountain, been up through the snow to Blackdome Mountain on a clear day, looked out over Lone Cabin gulch from up there, and seen all those mountains out to the south and southeast: China Head, Yalakom far to the south, French, Red, Poison, Buck, Quartz and massive Big Dog in the back, faraway Eldorado, Cardtable, Relay, Dash Hill, probably Mt. Warner above Warner Pass in behind to the southwest, maybe Elbow mountain above Lorna Lake, perhaps Mt. Vic on the edge of the Dil-dil Plateau, probably Taseko Mountain on the far end of the massif and Ts'yl-os for sure, by its inimitably lone self farther west. I swear I could see, past all those western, snowy-white mountains, as far as Niut Mountain, above Tatlayoko Lake, a long, long, hazy way away. I've looked across at Niut so many times from Iris Redford's cabin that I recognize that big rock wall and angled snow chute down the front of it; well, I think I'm sure I do.

I've been walking. I walked up Grinder Creek, saw the site of Grinder's old place there, dead-reckoned my way over the ridge to Two Cabin Lake, climbed up onto that rocky sheep refuge above it, communed a bit there with the gods, walked down into Wycott's place above Wycott Flats, and saw his old house and barn down there, all alone, in surprisingly intact condition after a century. And I've seen wild critters: wintering mule deer in large numbers all through those lower-elevation ranchlands, coyotes, black bears and a dark grizzly over by Stobie Lake. Chilco Choate says the dark ones are males; I could see by the grizzled hump it was male, a good size too, and in a hurry to leave. That "epic journey" feeling is beginning to set in, and it feels just about right for the Junction.

The morning is fresh and the birds are calling and flitting about; contented Hereford cows are grazing. I turn at the turnoff and pick my way down. The track is still a little wet, slick and rutted. Golden balsamroot sunflowers in patches shine bright, faces up; to a flower, in love with the sun. On the route down I stop at the cattle guard, haul out my single-bitted camp axe and pound and pare and flatten all possible pointy bits on that miserable edifice into submission, and then some, and continue on.

I park at the fence near Mitchell's memorial, where I had seen the young rams; pack my water, lunch, map and sunscreen; lace on my old walking boots; jam my hat on my head; and hoof on down the hill. From the high points I can see the place where the two great rivers meet, and I get some glimpses of the poplar grove where those house-pit kekuli holes that Grant Keddie talked about are purported to be.

By the bottom of the first steep hill, the sole of one boot has become separated. I carry on, flapping along through the, no doubt, tick-ridden big sagebrush. I sound like the "old Chinaman" in a story in John Steinbeck's *Cannery Row*, one of my favourite stories in one of my favourite books—the one where the brave, but thoughtless, young boy calls the old Chinese man, who comes flap-flap-flapping up from under the canneries along the low-tide shore, rude names. The old man turns and stares hard at the kid, and imparts

The Junction, looking south; the Chilcotin River enters the Fraser River from the northwest (the right). Photo courtesy of Peter Stein.

a fast vision to him of a place too sharp, too lonely, too total for the child to handle, forcing him to close his eyes, desist and turn away. Like me, the old man carries on, flap-flapping along his way.

No matter, the song sparrows and meadowlarks are singing, "singin' in the sage, just singin' in the sage," and sage buttercups are blooming. It's a good day to be alive and walking. I reach the last rock and clay bluffs above the final flats and the point, a short mile beyond; I can see Keddie's poplars, but the cliffs there are high and too steep for me. There are sheep trails cutting down here and there, but I'm no sheep. I am old enough to collect a pension, and my balance is less than it was. I'm alone here, and the sole is coming off one of my walking shoes. I prowl around the top of the rocks and hard clay, trying to find a way down, but there is nothing that feels reasonably safe.

There is a man named Doc in some smoky, dark room somewhere, wearing armbands and a green eyeshade, who's known to say in a wheezy voice, "You gotta know when to hold 'em, and when to fold 'em." Well, I'm not as rash as I used to be, and I fold 'em. I sit down for a drink of water and a bite and decide to walk back along the verge of the sagebrush flats above the Chilcotin River to the west and see what I can see down over the edge.

In a lone, tall fir on the brim of the canyon, I spot a slow-moving, greenish-backed bird, larger than the usual little brown sparrow types of the open grasslands, one I'm not used to seeing. After some creeping and peering, I reckon it to be a yellow-breasted chat of the warbler family, unusually silent (they are named appropriately and are typically noisy birds in springtime), well beyond its normal range and clearly not alarmed by me. From near the fir I watch the bird for a while, and in doing so I spy a pair of four-legged metal tripods, or "quarterpods": first one on the edge of the grass flat, and then another on a rocky, exposed sagebrush slope several hundred feet below me, put there years back by Keddie's "archy" crew, I deduce. They mark the way down to the kekuli dig site, around the corner out of sight, on the final flats and gravel beds near the trees down at the Junction.

But time is passing and that will be an adventure for a future day. I memorize the clues for the access route—two large fir trees spaced far apart, standing alone, each on the edge—and commence a quick march back through the sage and up the steep hillside at the end, deep-breathing and heart-pounding the last several hundred yards to the car on the lookout point by the monument. I catch my breath, do a final glassing of the coulees and breaks for hints of invisible horned life, drink some water, divest myself of those defunct boots and head for asphalt.

Those last bottom miles of the Junction car track are, in fact, a loop. I had come down the open western route with the wide views; I would return by the east side along the edge of the drop-off over the Fraser River, not far from where Simon Fraser and his crew made their near calamitous passage through Iron Rapids. I was hoping for vistas upriver and across to the big, open range country north of Alkali Lake Ranch, presumed by many, but not all, to be the oldest registered ranch in the region.

The prevailing heat at the Junction is on the west; the east side is steep but plainly retains more moisture than on the Chilcotin side. On top, the country is a pleasant mix of open fir forest and wide meadows. This latitude is too winter-cold for ponderosa pines; the northernmost ones on the entire continent had grown, typically large, over-age and beginning to rot, on an afternoon sun-facing hillside above the Gang Ranch bridge, much farther south. That was before the recent pine bark beetle outbreak killed them all off. Now, on the east side of the river, between the bridge and Canoe Creek, a distance of about five miles, there is not a single live ponderosa pine left standing, not one. The most northwesterly ponderosa that I have seen, and that I believe still exist, grow on open slopes up Gun Creek past Spruce Lake, north of far-off Gold Bridge.

My timing is perfection. All those meadows on the east side, acres of them, are seas of blooming balsamroot sunflowers, yellow gold as far as I can see, and I can see for miles upriver, at least as far as Ross Gulch. I think I recognize the open slopes north of the mouth of Riske Creek in my glasses; they are gold also, just discernible in the slanting light. The sun's rays are lowering, shining through flowers, millions of flowers, gold accentuating gold, casting golden shadows, no less golden for being shadows. These flowers are as lustrous as they will ever be, millions of faces turned up to the sky to the great shining source of it all, following it sinking slowly into the west. Those golden flowers are immaculate.

I shut off the motor and step out, my jaw probably hanging loose on my chest, and simply stand there. I have seen many spring sunflower shows in my time, always wondrous and welcome, but never like this. The world is sunshine, sunflowers and silence, except for that far faraway, almost not-there, sound of the big Fraser River, motionless as usual, 1800 feet below.

Eventually I climb back into my car and proceed slowly in a low gear; the Pathfinder runs quietly. I have gone only a few hundred feet at most when I come upon a mother black bear and a single small cub, close by the track. Mama bear is panicky and a bit indecisive; she is not large and looks and acts young. She finally opts for a low brush screen a few feet away from the road. Baby, a regular little dark fur ball, likely following old instructions, heads straight for a lone fir tree not far from me, crying, "Maaaaaa, what should

Arrow-leaved balsamroot, also known as spring sunflowers, blanket parts of the dry Interior grassland from late April to early June. Photo courtesy of Marne St. Claire.

I do? What should I do?" all the way. He sounds a little like a small sheep. He hesitates at the foot of the tree, looks at, or for, his mother once or twice, then scampers up about fifteen feet, fast, and waits, agitated.

Meanwhile, I can see Mama standing upright, watching me from behind her brush pile, huffing and puffing and uttering deep moans and groans, hoping to drive me off, a very worried look on her face. She has obviously been used to a quiet, slow-paced life down here at the Junction. I hear new sounds from a tall fir snag to my left, a good thirty feet up, and see three more, small fur balls come skittering and scraping down out of the top of it, they too uttering small choruses of "maaaaaaa," but not so panicked as the first cub. They race across and proceed up the same single fir tree as number one cub, and the four of them, with the alacrity of fat squirrels, climb to the extreme top, itself over thirty feet up. They hang there like four oversized bunches of grapes.

Well, what to do? Bear mother comes out from behind her scrim, worried, but dedicated to the end. I am really glad I am not on foot; Mother

A bear family, in this case a mother grizzly bear and cubs. Photo courtesy of Larry Travis, Raincoast Images, and Jane Woodland and Chris Genovali, Raincoast Conservation Foundation.

might have let her anxiety get the better of her, and of me. She is huffing and puffing and banging her jaws together with a loud hollow clicking sound, warning me to please keep my distance, she will fight if she needs to. All this is happening a mere sixty or seventy feet away from me. I indulge myself for another minute or two and then, after talking to her in my most reassuring tones, complimenting her on the good job she's doing, what fine-looking kids she's got, and what an unusually large family she has, I drive slowly away and stop farther up the track. Mum continues her huffing and moaning and jaw-banging, but with reduced intensity; then she decides she might as well climb that same standing fir as her kids. She manages about eight feet up the trunk to what looks like an uncomfortable perch between the cubs and the ground and waits, craning her head around to keep me in sight with that same alarmed expression, still ready for action if necessary. I can see the whites of her eyes. I back off some more, and my last, far view is of Mother plainly relaxing, and all five bears clambering slowly back down out of their refuge tree. Regular life can continue to go on as before down at the Junction.

I park to write notes. Woody Allen, that urban sage and backwoods seer, is correct: "Eighty percent of life is just showing up."

The rest is about perception and practice. Our senses can distract and fool us. Sometimes a place like the Junction can tell us there is more than what we may perceive at the moment, if we stay open and listen. Over time, especially with extended physical involvement, like walking, surfaces can become more manifestly illusory, and a sense of the underlying energy of a place, and the ages and changes that have affected it, becomes evident and difficult to ignore. That power may appear to be latent but it is only just, barely just. With a shift of seeing, we may perceive it as pulsing, ready to move, ready to change and massively powerful beyond all imagining. This is more true of the Junction than nearly all places I have experienced, something to do, I think, with its grandness and depth. It is like being on a mountaintop or high ridge; only, at the Junction, the perspective is into, not over, the rock and clay surface of the earth.

The Junction is much about light. The light at some of those dry, low-elevation sagebrush benches and slopes along the mid-Fraser is different; it has its own quality, especially in the heat and haze of summer, and can have something of a mirage impact on us. Marne has similar impressions: she has a particular awe of the Fraser River. She always has.

My times here in the Junction leave me, as always, with unfinished business: questions about place and soul and myth, perhaps; more questions about walking down, again, to that point above where the two rivers come together, that place where pre-contact aboriginal people and miners, Chinese and white, left their marks upon the land. I make my way through this life in a process of stages it seems: I see a place, revisit it, think about it, study it, read the maps and visit it again, perhaps in a different season when the light has changed and life responds accordingly. Each time is different. Each time I learn more; each time more questions arise, more answers emerge. I am part of a process, ongoing, a process much greater than me, with its own pace, not to be hurried: maybe next spring.

Then there is the tick bite. I picked up a tick down there, probably in the sagebrush as I passed through, branches brushing against me. It had started to bore into the small of my back when I apprehended it, and that pesky critter left me with a tiny ring of dead flesh and a minor health concern for a few months. I have a little reminder bump of our meeting, just above the belt line.

And more questions, especially one very basic one, that in pragmatic terms underlies all others in my view: namely, does this grand and varied land, this great set of regions that we find ourselves inhabiting out here in the West, belong to us or we to it? Or are we all simply one and the same, interconnected in ten thousand ways? This, as I see it, is a question of survival and the maturing of our culture, not to mention the preservation of lives and species. As well, it is a question of honour and, dare I say, best truth and good manners.

My answer might be, at this point in my understanding, that when we have been here long enough and paid attention to where we are, and the myth-stories start to come through us up out of this ground we walk on, when they demand to appear, unbidden, unshaped by our egos, individual and collective, and when their scratching at the walls of our minds and souls can no longer be ignored and we must stop everything, our involvements, our commitments, our grand ideas, in order to assist in their emergence, then we can say that perhaps we are growing up. We can begin to believe that we belong here.

There is another question: those fields of spring balsamroot sunflowers? Clearly they go on in their golden ways, reflecting and radiating the light of the sun as long as life and earth and seasons support. What I want to know is, and I hope and presume this is not a mere question of self: is their shining light just a bit more bright, if only a scintilla, for my having given them my utmost fullest attention for those few minutes, back there on that late afternoon at the brow of the canyon? Also, could the Fraser River far below, murmuring its faraway river sound, be in some way reciprocating the sunflowers' golden light? And could it be that the bear mother and her four cubs were listening? I saw a large elderly black bear once, in the backcountry of Banff National Park on an evening, sitting back against a stump at the roadside, his watery little eyes blinking, evidently enjoying the light of sunset, or at least taking in the warmth of the dying day. Perhaps our bear mama was busy teaching her young ones to be watchful as I happened by. It would take wild ignorance, or considerable life practice, to be certain of the answers.

WALKING TS'YL-OS: MOUNT TATLOW

The blue mountains are constantly walking.
—Master Dogen, 13th century

IN 1986, DON BROOKS AND I CLIMBED TO THE TOP OF MOUNT TATLOW, AS IT was then called, a monumental, snowy eminence of 10,058 feet overlooking Nemaiah Valley to the north. Tatlow stands largely alone. The peaks behind it are lower, less massive, less imposing, but even from as far away as the Chilcotin Highway west of Riske Creek, eighty miles to the northeast, Mount Tatlow stands dominant in the blue distance if the air is clear. Long stretches of gravel road in from Lee's Corner on the way to Nemaiah look to have been sighted exactly on the peak, a probable hint as to the route's history as a foot, horse and wagon trail through lodgepole pines without end.

Mount Tatlow has since reverted to its old name of Tsoloss or Ts'yl-os and is acknowledged as a living entity once again; the mountain has a considerable aura of mythos and power about it, or should I say "Him." Most of the mainly aboriginal residents of Nemaiah are careful to use restraint and appropriate decorum in referring to Ts'yl-os. Visitors might be wise to do the same. Like creatures of the wild, the great mountain does not like people to point or stare at him, so they say, and there is talk of consequences for those who do. What I am unsure of still is whether it is right to even refer to him by name. Am I being too direct, too presumptuous now in the telling of this story?

R.G. Tatlow, on the other hand, Vancouver financier and finance minister in Premier Richard McBride's Conservative government in the early years of the twentieth century, had a short-lived and significantly smaller impact on the world than Ts'yl-os. I suspect the honourable minister's concern for protocol would be limited to the appropriate use of titles. Staring and pointing would probably have been construed as simply the outcome of inferior upbringing, something to be expected in the colonies.

Stories, too, have energies and intentions of their own. I can tell you that after the usual wait for inclinations of story to emerge, due to the percolations and perambulations of time and mind and, I presume, spirit, this story of our dogged walk up the flanks of mighty Ts'yl-os fairly elbowed its way into my awareness. The story has been many years in the steeping. Finally, I had little choice but to sit down at the keyboard and begin. Ts'yl-os, a mountain being of limited patience, it seems, had had enough of waiting and was prodding the story into action.

Ts'yl-os and his wife, Eniyud, were given to arguing and mean-spiritedness, so the tales from distant myth time go. Eniyud, obviously overwrought at one point, thrust the baby onto his lap, left the two oldest kids for him to keep an eye on, swept up the rest of the children and moved on over by Tatlayoko Lake where, as Niut Mountain, she sits, their jagged offspring lined up behind her. They look severe and moody even now. Ts'yl-os, his ex-consort, Eniyud, and their progeny eventually turned to rock. You can see the two larger, older children tucked in behind Ts'yl-os, and the infant in his lap, but mind your manners; be sure not to be careless or offhand, and please do not point. Even the youngest child looks rough and tough.

The reputation of Ts'yl-os does perplex me, though. I can understand that the fracas and the responsibility of child-rearing might leave him in a bad mood. He has a powerful influence over the climate they say. The local weather is frequently blustery and changeable: dangerous winds come up suddenly from out of the peaks and ridges to the south and southwest and blow down the long lakes, Taseko, Tatlayoko and especially Chilko. There is a story of a Tsilhqot'in man up on a mountain who sighted invaders on a raft, Kwakwaka'wakw from the coast, moving down Chilko Lake, and who called on a great wind to destroy them. Ts'yl-os stands on the edge of the Chilcotin Plateau, and with the heightening of each summer day, the warming Interior air rises. Cold winds from off the shining glaciers and snowfields beyond the lakes, in the heart of the Coast Mountains, rush in to fill the void. Nemaiah Valley below Ts'yl-os is often windy, and exposed trees grow slowly with a gnarled list to leeward.

But, and I say this with as much respect as I can muster, according to the stories that come down to us, this massive mountain eminence is unduly touchy, perhaps even pushy, certainly hard to get along with. All mountains have their moods, but

Ts'yl-os is in the back; Peter Stein is in the foreground, on Tsoloss Ridge above Nemaiah Valley. Photo courtesy of John Schreiber.

Ts'yl-os stands out—though I have heard that to be edgy or offensive near or to Eniyud when she is in an off mood brings on a wrath with a stormy, some might say mean, edge that is unparalleled. I remind myself that these are mountain-gods we are talking about here, a world I know little of, so these years I back away with deference, eyes and mind averted, mutter a quick acknowledgment—not too intense, not too dismissive—and carry on.

Perhaps the issue is simply that, however mighty, Ts'yl-os is a wild being in a wild, subtle and sensitive world, and like all denizens of the wild, and like "wild" itself, he requires an appropriately respectful approach, a light touch. Perhaps a point or stare is simply too aggressive and causes even

Niut (Eniyud) Mountain, former consort of Ts'yl-os, and their offspring, above the northwest end of Tatlayoko Lake. Photo courtesy of Marne St. Claire.

a mountain to flinch, to withdraw, like small birds circling imperceptibly to the back of the bush the moment you focus your binoculars on them. Maybe Ts'yl-os is the mountain equivalent of a wolverine or grizzly bear and simply needs to be left alone.

In August 1984, before Don and I made our slow way up Ts'yl-os, we drove south, off the long and dusty Nemaiah road, to the mouth of the Tchaikazan (Tsichessaan) River Valley at the top end of Taseko Lake. From there we walked up the river, which was flowing in its customarily uproarious manner out of a mass of glaciers in the southwest, most notably Monmouth and Tchaikazan. The 1:50,000 topo map of the headwaters of the Tchaikazan and the Lord River farther east, in the heart of the Coast Range—a desolate and unexpectedly lifeless and spooky place that Don and I ventured into laboriously by canoe in 1990—is mainly alpine white. The maps differentiate a bluish white for glaciers and thin brown contour lines on white for peaks, treeless

Rock and glacier country up the Tchaikazan River. Photo courtesy of John Schreiber.

rock, tundra and sub-alpine terrain; forest green is minimal. The Tchaikazan trip was our first foray into that wild and chilly region.

We walked as far as Goetz's Cabin below Spectrum Pass, where we camped for a few days. The river was high and muddy after half a summer of snow and ice melt, and water was backed onto the trail in places. There were few sand and gravel bars visible, and where the trail followed them we had to cut into the bush. We came upon clean-edged, long-clawed grizzly tracks in damp earth in several places, notably the trail beneath our feet. The weather was mostly overcast and rainy; the hanging glaciers on the southwest side of the valley were half hidden in cloud, and we had to work to stay warm.

The next day we climbed up onto the pass for a look down into Dorothy Lake and the Yohetta route on the far side, and to see if we could spot upper Chilko Lake. On our way, we spied a mule deer doe and her fawn sneaking along a gully below us. A small herd of bucks were bunched together on the snowfields above, escaping the bugs, and a cluster of mountain goats in a hurry, not their typical pace, made a fast retreat across the sloped open tundra below RCAF Peak. They obviously knew what it was to be hunted by two-leggeds and were taking no chances. On our way back down, at the edge of the drop-off, we found goat wool hanging in strands on stunted alpine fir trees, like faded Tibetan prayer flags waving in the wind. This was where the goat herd had been feeding and shedding early in the season when the snow line was still low. Don collected wool samples for his two young daughters.

When we reached the valley bottom, I stopped to kneel in moss at the edge of the little creek, chuckling its way down beside us, to splash water on my face. Something in that cold, clear, wet, moment has stayed with me, pungent to this day.

Goetz's Cabin is situated at a big bend in the valley where the Tchaikazan is especially wide and braided. At the end of each day, if the rain wasn't too bad, I meditated, hunkered into my Gore-Tex coat, on a rock out in a dry meadow in front of the cabin. A doe would come out of the buckbrush across the river to feed in the late afternoon, her fawn hidden, scentless and curled into itself back in the scrub timber. She glanced over occasionally, and I wondered if she was using the proximity of the cabin for cover.

We drank hot, overproof rums in the evenings. In those days we carried fresh limes, nutmeg or cinnamon, brown sugar, and butter squeezed from a plastic tube. Once, years before in the Rainbow Mountains, Don and I stood at dusk outside our campsite with half-consumed drinks in hand and slightly crooked grins, watching a big bull caribou with full antler rack trot by us in the gloom. We had been route finding by compass bearings across rolling alpine tundra that day, a gloriously free way to travel. On an old rock slide on the far side of a gentle pass, the route coalesced briefly into a tidy, unexpectedly level trail, the rock slabs worn and shifted most elegantly into position by generations of wear from those big caribou hooves.

One rainy day we walked up the river to the snout of Tchaikazan Glacier, crossing the outlets of the several small glaciers on our side of the valley, Friendly and Miserable Glaciers among them. Each creek was steep and on a rampage, and we had a tough job crossing them. We passed the Alpine Club base campsite, looking weather-beaten already, and made our way up the mile or so of barren outwash plain and lateral moraines to the ice front; most of the plain was still without plant life, the glacier having retreated so recently. The ice was twenty feet thick or more at its margin, and propped up in a newly stacked rock pile just in front was an ice axe with a helmet hanging off it. This was a monument to a young climber who, while roping up farther along the glacier, backed onto a snow-covered crevice and fell to his death.

Of course the day warmed, the rain and meltwater increased, and on the way back we found, not to our surprise, that the glacial side creeks had risen sharply. We were wading in white water—ice only minutes before—that reached the tops of our thighs. Don carried our small axe in his big pack, and we cut ourselves a solid fir staff to be used as a third leg, each of us in turn, to reduce the chances of a quick tumble into oblivion. That short, sub-alpine, krummholz brush was as impenetrable as any upcoast salal jungle, and the pole we cut was almost as dense, hard and old as the boulders we were clambering over; the axe, filed sharp, bounced when we trimmed it.

> *We cut ourselves a solid fir staff to be used as a third leg, each of us in turn, to reduce the chances of a quick tumble into oblivion.*

Goetz had recently bought the cabin from Johnny Blatchford, an old-time guide-outfitter from down at Tsuniah Lake off Chilko, and he had boarded the window from bears and removed the door knob, somewhat inhospitably we thought, from people like us. Goetz was originally from overseas and apparently did not fully appreciate the old Chilcotin values of an open cabin in bad weather or the free use of traditional trails in wild places. On a cold, wet, late afternoon a day or two earlier, we split a piece of kindling to fit the slot where the shaft of the missing door handle had been, turned it to release the latch and open the door, and spent a pleasantly warm, dry evening inside. Before we left, we reboarded, wrote a grateful note, locked up and departed the valley.

On the way out, we picked up our stash of cold beer, a pair of O'Keefe "High Tests," from a side-creek pool not far from the car, a time-honoured

J S and Don Brooks at Goetz's Cabin up the Tchaikazan River in 1984. We may have been enjoying hot rums that evening. Photo courtesy of Don Brooks.

and nourishing end-of-trail ritual. Camping that evening at Big Lake on the edge of the Chilcotin plateau, away from the mountains, we saw that not a drop of rain had fallen out there; the ground was dust.

That night I awoke to a juvenile coyote's howl next to a corner of our tent, then a low, measured, adult answering howl from farther off. In my half-consciousness, I heard the conversation, the tone of it, clearly. Junior had yipped in his high-pitched, coyote-pup voice, "Wow, Mum, lookit what I found here, eh!" Mother had answered in a slow, low-pitched howl, the archetypical call of all worried mothers, "Watch it, son. It's a pair of those dangerous and tricky two-leggeds I've been warning you about. Get out of there fast if you know what's good for you."

In the morning, the story was all there to read in the campsite dust. Junior's footprints a few feet away, coming and going, and Mum's much larger tracks, including her butt-end markings where she'd sat waiting for him a hundred feet off by a brushed-in bend in the track. We knew there must be a den close by. I have a memory of a bright, sharp-edged moon that night, low and large in the sky above Ts'yl-os, and long, pointed tree shadows on the ground.

For decades, I've dipped in a passing way into the world of Trickster and the ephemeral, difficult-to-define nature of myth-mind. I have long held the conviction that Trickster Coyote, in all his many incarnations around the world—Raven, of course, and Mink, Blue Jay, Br'er Rabbit, Spider, Praying Mantis, Reynard the fox, and all the rest of that pantheon out of the land of myth—in his persistent self-absorption and his oblivious isolation, is too much like our modern, linear conception of ego to be an accident. He is a foxy, creative, destructive, irresponsible, horny, greedy, often funny fool, like ego, and every bit as deceiving, especially of himself. "Egotist pure and simple" is the corroborating phrase anthropologist Franz Boas uses in his introduction to James Teit's book on Nlaka'pamux (Thompson) Indian traditions.

Coyote has an unfailing way of outsmarting himself, then picking himself up and, unlike Humpty Dumpty—but just like ego—putting himself back together again, after even the most debilitating of disasters. In his many escapades, Coyote has lost more body parts than a regiment of Crimean War veterans and, amazingly, he seems always to get them attached and back in working order in time for his next scheme or impulse. No matter what, Coyote insists on being heard and seen and taking part—often for me in that hazy crack in consciousness at the first light of day or those last crepuscular moments before nightfall.

But Coyote is more than a cunning, wily, bumbling and fantastically, and usually canny, creative fool. He comes down to us from the times of the animal-gods, those olden-day myth times when animals informed us and helped us to become human. Coyote and his ilk appear to have been an essential, near-eternal presence in older times, a persistent reminder to us still—if we choose to look—that we are part of the animal world. Beneath the modern, civilized masks we wear, our wild, shadowy, animal nature endures, manifesting the shift from our older, primal selves to the self-reflective, ego-based beings we are now. Above all else, Trickster/Coyote is wild, beyond our control. Karl Kerenyi writes that Trickster exhibits "his true nature as …the spirit of disorder, the enemy of boundaries."

In "The Incredible Survival of Coyote," an essay in *The Old Ways*, Gary Snyder says "Coyote Old Man. Not that he's 'old' now, in white-man times, but that he's always been old. Not the oldness of history, but the oldness of 'once upon a time'—outside history; in Dream Time, which surrounds us. And out of 'Dream Time' comes the healing."

Snyder concludes by saying: "We slip those masks a bit to the side, and see there Coyote/Man the Trickster; Bear/Man King of the Mountains; Deer/Mother, Queen of Compassion. In turn those Type-Beings, Mind-created, Earth-created, are again masks. The Shining One peeks out from behind a boulder and is gone—is always there."

Two years later, Don and I walked slowly up the slopes of Mount Tatlow, or Ts'yl-os, still unaware of who or what we were dealing with. We had minor pretensions to actual climbing then, and the top of Tatlow was steep snow and ice. The upper end of Nemaiah Valley sits close to 4000 feet; so we had over 6000 feet of elevation to ascend to reach the peak—not a major deal for the congenitally rugged, but plenty for us. We would each carry an extra five to ten pounds of climbing gear in case we needed it.

We followed the long road in from Lee's Corner, parked our vehicle in thick brush off the road, laced up our boots and circled about to be sure of the right route. Then we started the slow plod up the hill. At first the route followed a grown-in Cat trail, originally a firebreak but later used for an access to summer cattle range and for hunting by the Purjue Brothers and their descendants. A younger Purjue had, as part of his guiding business, a hunting cabin up on Tsoloss Ridge, though it had recently been burned out. It was a warm August afternoon. We passed a couple of happy horses—domestic stock, friendly and recently footloose—slowly grazing their way up the hillside into high country. That evening we found the remains of the Purjue cabin a short distance up the creek from our campsite, the grass already growing green and tall over charred wood, rusted chimney pipe, tin cans and stove bits. Here, the question of possible First Nations "land claims" issues

Coyote. Photo courtesy of Damon West Photography.

intrudes, inescapably. Did the cabin just burn, or did it *get* burnt? Or did Ts'yl-os simply find the shack offensive, an eyesore and blight, and any handy means of removing it from his person would do?

For dinner that night we had steak, roasted over glowing fir bark–coals, and thickly smeared in Stilton cheese-butter, with potatoes slow-baked in tinfoil by the edge of the fire, and a dressed green salad on the side. A pair of great horned owls began their "who's awake me too—who's awake me too" calls, back and forth, echoing across the wet-meadow, swamp-birch creek bottom below us. That old "high lonesome" feeling was starting to set in. Alpenglow lit up the mountain, which stood there—still as stone—a great glowing silent mass above us.

In the morning, after a full breakfast, we hoisted our now somewhat lighter packs, carried on across Tsoloss Creek at a place where the gully wasn't too steep, and caught up to those two horses again in close sub-alpine brush, predominately soopalallie and false mountain azaleas. The animals were even

Campsite at Big Lake with Ts'yl-os in the far distance. Don Brooks is preparing another fine meal in wilderness. Photo courtesy of John Schreiber.

more easygoing than before and were definitely working their way toward the expanse of open alpine on the east side of the mountain, perhaps to join wild relatives up there. I had heard there were wild horses up on Tatlow, mostly on those mid-elevation slopes at the headwaters of Elkin Creek. We were all trail pals by this time, and Don and I rubbed their broad, dusty rumps as we squeezed past them.

We headed south, then veered right at the divide and picked a route across a long, boulder-strewn, sparsely treed sidehill to the southwest, aiming toward ponds at the base of some distinctively shaped snowfields we had spotted on the drive in. Our packs were still heavy, and picking our way across that mossy boulder field was slippery and hazardous.

Don and I camped at 6500 feet, behind scrubby alpine firs next to a narrow, snow-fed tarn. The area had been grazed by stock in past years, and old, desiccated dung was banked up under the trees. They had obviously served as a windbreak and/or cud-chewing stop for passing animals. Our dinner that evening was semi-dried barbequed pork and rice with fresh herbs and diced green pepper, concocted, as usual, by Don, the king of the backpacker cooks.

It was warm and still up on the mountain, and the view north and northeast across the wide Chilcotin was vast and blue, with the rolling plateau, a few bright lakes reflecting sky here and there, and shades of deepening dusty smoky reds over the far northwestern mountains. Night lowered its blanket across the land, and a single light flashed somewhere to the northeast, once only; it evoked for me lonely memories of solitary navigation lights flashing in the dark when I was a youth on boat voyages home along Johnstone Strait off Vancouver Island. Always those lights reminded me of Mathew Arnold's "Dover Beach," and the lines I studied in school—"*the light gleams, and is gone/... The Sea of Faith/Was once, too, at the full.../...[and now] ignorant armies clash by night.*"

At four in the morning we woke up sick. I was raised on upcoast, cedar-swamp water, brown like weak tea at runoff times, and a touch fishy in autumn salmon season; consequently I have an iron gut and was merely afflicted with an upset stomach and a deep lassitude. But poor old Donny had the full-blown, head-down dry heaves that carried on well into the day. We spent the afternoon lying about limply in the shade, sleeping and, if awake, feebly cursing the barbecued pork, the presumed cause of our misery. I was to learn later, after the trip and a little homework, that a slurry of fire ashes and water, ingested, might have provided us with a base antidote for our acid innards. In later years, with hindsight and increased insight, I grew to wonder if perhaps we'd been staring too hard at old Ts'yl-os, thinking judgmental or insulting thoughts or, in some other way, carelessly offending his mythy dignity. We really didn't know who Ts'yl-os was in those early days. He had given us few clues.

We were still weak the next morning when we began our final walk up Tatlow's great, rounded shoulder, above the snowbanks. It was a long, grinding, near-monotonous walk, but for the startling blue of the clear sky up there, and the incredible views in all directions but the one under our feet. While I walked, I found myself meditating on some opening lines of the *Mountains and Rivers Sutra* by Master Dogen, Soto Zen Buddhist teacher of the thirteenth century. Or was it the verses that fixated on me? I had first heard them through Gary Snyder: "The blue mountains are constantly walking. The stone woman gives birth to a child in the night... He who doubts that the mountains walk does not yet understand his own walking."

As I trudged and mulled, the smaller peaks southeast and south of Tatlow, which I now believe to be the older offspring of Eniyud and Ts'yl-os, were elevating and lowering themselves according to the undulations of the mountainside we were treading upon, up and down, slowly up and down, behind the immediate ridge in front of us. That skyline was sharper than a knife edge honed fine: rock and snow on blue. I tried to intuit, in my near-blank way, how they could possibly be "walking." I could see that the two toothy humps of rock moved as much or more than me, up and down and sideways, seemingly of their own volition, like great whales surfacing and sinking. To the degree that I was not looking at myself, the mountains moved.

I have always been mesmerized by skylines whetted to infinity. There is never a line so fine, so sharp, as that line between sky and a mountain ridge in thin, clear, high-altitude air, particularly when the ridgeline is long and the sky has turned that deep, high-country, ultramarine blue of early dusk, say, or after a clean rain or quick summer snowfall.

There is a saying from Haida Gwaii: *The world is as sharp as the edge of a knife*. For me, this statement has always been evocative of skylines and the pure flowing form lines in the best Northwest Coast aboriginal art, as exemplified by, among others, two particularly fine artists: the great Robert Davidson (Haida) and Art Thompson (Nuu-chah-nulth), now deceased. The statement seems to be about the hard-edged dangers of existence and the constant need for fully focused awareness in life. These years I hear the saying as a keen observation on the acute differences in the intrinsic nature and meaning of all things.

There is a saying from Haida Gwaii: The world is as sharp as the edge of a knife.

I have wondered sometimes if—to Haida, Nuu-chah-nulth and other coast peoples immersed in sea space—this observation might refer as well to that fine, far-off line where the blue-grey North Pacific Ocean meets the blue-grey sky, an edge so fine those two great spaces sometimes merge into one.

In the text of *Mountains and Rivers Sutra*, there is a useful clue to note: "The blue mountains are neither sentient nor insentient; the self is neither

134

sentient nor insentient. Therefore we can have no doubts about these blue mountains walking."

For myself, I am maybe sure about one thing. The knowing here is about intrinsic truth: the intrinsic truth of blue mountains, of every sentient and insentient body in existence, including that busy, doughty Bewick's wren I observe in our Victoria backyard. It is a resident there and, with its partner, lives an active, purposeful life in the shrubs and trees along our fence lines. The female of the couple nests occasionally in the bow of our upside-down canoe in springtime. In one of those clear moments of grace we are given occasionally, I knew the bird to be Bewick's wren, inimitably, absolutely, nothing less: the Buddha-nature of wren, a glimpse—a quick sense of the Buddha-nature of all beings upon this earth, animate or otherwise.

We are all walking, constantly it seems—the blue mountains, Bewick's wrens, all of us, like the ages passing. The other day I remarked on Dogen's amazing opening sentences to my partner, Marne: "I don't get that second line, 'The stone woman gives birth to a child in the night,'" I said. "What on earth does he mean?"

"That's easy," she replied, busy, but forbearing as always. "Stone woman is Eniyud, giving birth to all those kids." Perhaps it takes a mother—these intuitions are simple when you begin at the beginning.

Don and I ground our way up to the top by early afternoon and stopped for lunch. The pitch got steeper and we had to kick or dig toeholds in the hard snow. We only reached the first, slightly lower peak. There were several hundred feet of steep snow cornices and the icy, near-vertical mother of all drop-offs—an incredibly long way down, most of the mountain actually— between us and the primary peak. Extremely steep places make me queasy. There was no way I would attempt to go over there, not with those over- hanging cornices. I was perfectly happy where I was, nestled into a snow hole, eating my bread and cheese up there in an infinity of snow and sky.

It was an exceptionally warm, calm day. Ts'yl-os stood alone, dozing I would think. We sat and munched and looked out at the big wide world around us, while little flocks of small twittering birds flew by overhead. What

American poet Gary Snyder and friends at Hollyhock, Cortes Island, BC, 1985. Fraser Lang, now deceased, from the Yalakom Valley, stands behind Gary; JS is on the left. Photo courtesy of Fred Zwegat and Gary Ronjak.

else could they be doing up there, at over 10,000 feet in thin air, but having fun? They could have easily flown by at a lower elevation, but they didn't. Perhaps they are drawn skyward to the light, like Don the scientist and me, for the same reason I walk in these wild places and write: to get as close as I can to light. I believe those birds, looking down at us, must have been astounded to spot these new, arresting, Gore-Tex–clad additions to Ts'yl-os's windblown exterior. This is how legends begin.

On our last night out, down on Tsoloss Ridge, the horned owls were still hooting across to each other in the cool evening air. We listened. The mountain watched. The following fresh morning, after we swabbed the late-August dew off the tent and packed up, we stood looking at the great sun-shiny mountain, an extended pause before hoisting our near-depleted packs to shoulder and heading back down the hill. As we scanned, we spotted movement up there above tree line on the northern slope. Wild horses were feeding in low brush, about two dozen of them—sorrels, bays, blacks, greys, roans, coyote duns, their bodies glistening, their tails and manes twitching in the morning sun; the shadows were still long. The horses were on a fast graze moving west across the mountainside, feeding and moving, being horses. They exuded a deep restless energy. Animals keep on informing us, same as in the old myth-time days, if we show up and pay close attention. They have not ceased. Nothing has changed.

Coyote, in all his forms, natural, mythic, tricky, has always been here. The blue mountains still constantly move. Is there anything, anywhere, that is not wild?

AN ASCENSION OF CRANES

The most beautiful experience we can have is
the mysterious.
It is the fundamental emotion which stands
at the cradle of true art and true science.
　　　　—Albert Einstein, "The World as I See It"

IN THIS BEAUTIFUL PROVINCE WE INHABIT, THERE IS A VALLEY DOWN BY THE border, down on that southern medicine line running long and straight between us and the USA, called the Similkameen. A fast mountain river, not lengthy—a hundred miles, more or less—runs through it. "Similkameen" (Smalqmixw) means "the eagle people" in the language of the aboriginal inhabitants of the region, so as the name implies, the valley, the river and the folks who live there, and who have done so for millennia, are synonymous; they are one and the same. The river is without salmon now, since the building of a dam on the lowest reaches just above Oroville in Washington State, but they did swim up here once upon a time, according to local lore and myth-stories.

　　In these modern times, this valley has become another of those semi-forgotten places that abound throughout our land, where the inhabitants carry on, and travellers don't stop much but pass through on their way to somewhere else: points east, places where urgent issues induce and intrude, urban places.

Similkameen River near Hedley in southern British Columbia. Photo courtesy of John Schreiber.

The Similkameen River, too, carries on in that marvellous and underappreciated way of all rivers in this country. Its flow is relentless. It has run always, in its own manner, day and night, four seasons of the year, since the glaciers. It may flood muddy and wild, it may ebb clean and clear as new glass, it may freeze over in places, but the river runs, as rivers of the northwest do, seemingly forever. We all of us—humans, river beaver, otters, trout fry, damselflies, mergansers and harlequin ducks, even deer and elk—count, absolutely, on its certainty.

The river rises high on the lee side of the wet Cascade Mountains. It flows southeast, then north, and drops fast, rock-flour green and stony, to Princeton and the old mines, mills and workings along there: Whipsaw Creek, Copper Mountain, Allenby, Blackfoot and all the rest. Just past Princeton, where the Tulameen, the "red earth" (ochre) river, joins from the west, and under the grassy slopes of (Bill) Miner Mountain, otherwise known as Bald Mountain, the Similkameen veers to the southeast again. It keeps on, straight and fast, below the ancient north-side trail, past numerous red ochre rock-painting panels and boulders sited in overlooking, sun-facing places along the track where pedestrian and equestrian travellers in pre-contact times could not miss them. With the coming of the gold miners in the 1850s and '60s, the pictograph trail became the Hedley stagecoach road and, a hundred years after that, the route for a natural-gas pipeline.

From this stretch on, the valley bottom is a mix of domesticity and wild, a strip of verdant green: clematis and cottonwoods, hayfields and grazing cattle, and enclosing, thinly wooded, rocky mountain walls, streaked talus slopes and precipitous bunchgrass hillsides. This is bighorn sheep or mountain goat territory, according to the degree of steepness and access to escape terrain. The river continues its descent past the orchards and market gardens, vineyards and produce stands of Keremeos and Cawston. It does a long S turn all the while, slowing and flowing south now in curly bends and swampy oxbows to the US border. Below Hedley, and especially past Keremeos, the valley is big sagebrush land.

By the time the river crosses that imaginary forty-ninth latitude line splitting north from south, Canuck from Yankee, and separating our two rather different settler cultures, the low country is sunburned semi-desert. It joins its main valley stem, the Okanagan River (spelled Okanogan in the US), at Oroville. The last miles of the Similkameen are characterized by rough water and, on the lower flats and slopes, antelope bush or "greasewood," an angular, spiky-looking shrub with a very limited range on the Canadian side. The presence of antelope bush is an intimation of the great, dry, Interior Basin country stretching over 1200 miles south to Mexico. There are occasional large guys in big hats in this southern country, unhurried men wearing suspenders and pointy-toed boots. Should they happen to speak, you hear accents and attitudes surprisingly different from those of many of their northern cousins. The rivers prevail and carry on, and their combined waters flow past naturally bone-dry but irrigated ground, through the Channeled

Scablands, site of one of the greatest floods of all known geologic time, down to the Columbia and the wide open ocean far beyond.

The first and only village the Similkameen River passes on the American side is a tiny collection of half-abandoned houses and thoroughly abandoned mine workings called Nighthawk—that name has the flavour of a fifties black-and-white western movie about it. Farther along are more sun-blackened old buildings, piles of rusted junk and machinery parts, corroded graffiti-marked concrete, and holes in the ground called, in earlier, more lively times, Okanogan City, Ruby, and Loomis to the south.

Just above the line on the BC side is little Chopaka (*c'upaq*, which translates as "the breast of the mountain," the place where "the last light of the day shines"), a favoured place, a place to gladden the heart: willow bottoms, sloughs and grown-in hayfields, scattered houses and the odd log barn situated along the road. Horses and deer, stotting mulies and bounding whitetails both, and small flocks of Canada geese fatten up on the low ends of those fields. There are beaver in the backwaters; sharp-eyed hawks in tall trees, watching; big sage and sumac on the dry edges and hillsides; and bitterroot in the rocky places, blooming deep pink in May. Spring green comes early here compared to upriver and most of the rest of the provincial Interior. Some of the northering bird species seem exotic: lark sparrows, catbirds, lazuli buntings, bobolinks, occasional fly-catching Lewis woodpeckers, even rare sage thrashers on sagebrush flats a couple of miles east.

A favoured place, a place to gladden the heart: willow bottoms, sloughs and grown-in hayfields, scattered houses and the odd log barn situated along the road.

Chopaka is one of those end-of-the-side-road places, a place you cannot pass through, a place you do not hear about. It was never known much, except to aboriginal folks in the old days, maybe liquor smugglers during prohibition and the odd dope trafficker now.

This land is mainly Indian land, First Nations reserve land, along the Similkameen on the southwest side from Chopaka up past the Ashnola River

Lower Similkameen River at the bridge to Chopaka. Photo courtesy of John Schreiber.

mouth as far as Hedley, and the fertile riparian edges and eco-diversity of the area have benefited for that. The relatively natural state of much Indian land—sagebrush slopes, hayfields and wetlands mostly—provides something of a counterbalance, so far, to all those herbicides and pesticides from earlier, less-sensitive times in some saturated orchard grounds. There is something of a historic residue here, also, in the squared log buildings, settling and crumbling: the small white church on the knoll at ChuChuwayha, the cemeteries, the signs and memories of the old-time ranching world and the railroad right-of-way from the mines around Hedley and Princeton down into the US. The rails and creosote ties are scavenged and mostly gone; the Great Northern Railway station house, visible below the highway up from Chopaka (if you knew where to look), was still partially standing only a few years ago.

There is a quiet in this valley, a sense of time stopped, a sense of place you can slice, a depth of stillness not found in most peopled places. The river flows on, winding and bending: blackbirds rest by cattail ponds, marsh wrens buzz and flit, flycatchers perch and chase, kestrels stalk the fields and road edges, snakes warm themselves on rock ledges, butterflies flutter, sun-facing talus slopes bake and shimmer. People around here drive slowly, close gates and look up to see how the clouds are changing and if they can predict rain. The western mountains, hanging close above the valley, cast long, dark shadows each late afternoon, whether the day is bright or dull. Down here the elements have worn in, and the natural whole is far greater than the sum of the parts.

The first folks at Chopaka were Okanagan-speaking people; only a small number of elders speak it these days, although there are efforts in the schools now to teach the children. Okanagan is one of the Interior Salishan languages, an extensive linguistic family with wide variations and several dialects, ranging from the Secwepemc (Shuswap) in central BC to the Spokane, Coeur d'Alene and others in eastern Washington and northern Idaho, and the Se'lic (Flathead) peoples in western Montana, a buffalo culture once (from whom the word "Salish" originated). The people up the Similkameen River spoke a slightly different dialect, some say older, than the Okanagans and were connected via a small, now extinct Dene group, the Stuwi'x, to the Sce'exmx (Nicola Valley) people around Merritt. There are family links between the two areas to this day.

The Okanagan First Nation's culture straddles the forty-ninth parallel; a third of the people, approximately, live on the Canadian side, as far north as Douglas Lake and Vernon. The remaining two-thirds live south of the line, centred around Colville in northeastern Washington, although the reality for most aboriginal people here is that the border is not important; rather, it is like a mirage, a fantasy from another culture. James Teit from Spences Bridge, the eminent lay-ethnographer of a century ago, tells us that the Okanagans (and the Ktunaxa, or Kutenai, in the Kootenay River valley) were the first of the aboriginal cultures north of the line and west of the Rockies to use horses with any frequency. They obtained them through trade with other Salishan-speaking groups farther south and east not long before the arrival of the first Europeans to the area.

In our last employed years, Marne and I had been in the habit of going to the Similkameen for a quick taste of early spring in the southern Interior grasslands and for the sheer, dry beauty of the place; also, the valley never seemed to change much. We went there to smell the sagebrush, listen for meadowlarks, spot the first bluebirds and sage buttercups, and look for elk around Princeton and white goats on the cliffs by Keremeos. The Similkameen Valley, though limited in extent, is the nearest open grass and sagebrush land we can readily reach from the southwest coast where we live. By March, the grey damp of late winter in Victoria would get to us and we became restless.

We visited the valley on an Easter weekend not too long ago. We had driven up past Barcelo Road above Cawston to see birds in the open sage and along the brushed bottom of Blind Creek, high with snowmelt, tumbling down off Orofino Mountain. At a turnout facing southwest overlooking the valley, we stopped the car for a break and a fresh hit of cool, clear Similkameen air, and to look more closely for signs of liveliness. It was about high noon. We had a good view of the reclining maiden, Lady Chopaka, just over the border line, on the high ridge edge above the Similkameen River winding south away from us. She lies high above the streaked, sharp-angled talus slides, above even the snow and tree line, reposing on that western ridge down there in America, her snowy hair flowing fancifully, her stone breast, perfectly conical, pointed at the highest possible part of the sky. She left her first love for another, then died, and was laid out up on the ridge, so the old story goes. Her first love came to sit by her side, where he too died. The reclining maiden is a well-known figure locally, a regular member of the pantheon of important personages, past and present, in and around Cawston and Keremeos, and local citizens feel they must point her out to you.

High cirrus clouds were moving in from the west and the air was hazy, the sun muted but shining; frost from the morning's early shadowy places was twinkling. We stepped out onto cold gravel. Small brown birds twittered anonymously in the leafless willow thickets. The whips of the willows had reddened and thickened with the impending season, and our feet on pebbles made a crunching sound.

We heard the birds in the brush and our own feet, and after a moment we heard something more: a distant gabbling sound; a sound we had heard before

Similkameen Valley below Blind Creek and south of Cawston. Photo courtesy of John Schreiber.

in our lives, not infrequently, but always memorably, always breath and heart stopping; a massed sound, distant, directionless, that, after a minute or two of looking up and around and behind us, we discerned could only be coming from very high in the sky. The noon air was still sharp on our upraised faces.

At first we saw nothing, even after gazing and peering into the pale emptiness. Then Marne spotted them hundred of yards up; she seems to see such small, faraway things quickly. I spent several more slow seconds adjusting my own limited vision to finally spot them myself. It wasn't easy. They were pale and sky-like in colour to me, and just about invisible in the near-white sky, shape and colour shifting in and out of vision; for Marne they were dark. As I shifted and adapted my focus, the high emptiness seemed to fill with passing birds, dots, dots and more dots with slow-moving wings, barely discernible, dozens, hundreds at a time, methodically winging their way north.

They fly in a long, broad stream of loose, straggling vees, one after the other, vee after vee after wavering vee of great birds winging and gabbling and talking their way up the valley. They come out of the south, from far beyond and far above the range of our sight, from empty space into existence, it seems. From nothingness to substance: wild sandhill cranes.

The sight and trumpeting sound of several thousand migrating sandhill cranes...once you hear that sound you will not forget it. Their low, musical, rattling call is unique, inimitable, ages old and as immutable as the mountains and moving rivers.

It was still lightly sunny and slowly warming in this south-facing basin where we were standing. And as we stretched our bodies back and around to include the view of the ridge behind us, we saw the great flocks of calling, talking birds, thirty, fifty, a hundred or more to a flock, beginning to turn and wheel and catch the thermal in its morning rise off the heating hillside, ascending pretty much straight up above us and slightly to the west. To the north, higher up, more birds, the tiniest of dots, disappearing, evaporating into the high endless.

One by one the cranes break from their formations and veer slowly up into a great, loose, vertical spiral that, from above or straight below, would be seen to be turning clockwise. They turn in the same direction that air flows off a high-pressure weather cell, crossing the Pacific Ocean to us from central Asia according to the turn of the earth, and signalling clear skies and sunshine. As they gain altitude, the birds cease the powerful wing strokes that brought them here so far, assume up-tilted body positions, spread their wings wide, and begin a series of minor wing shifts, slight changes of posture, constantly, varyingly, adjusting their curl and curve so as to catch the maximum uplift from the thermal pressure gathering beneath. Collectively their bodies appear as a mass of small wobbles, micro-adaptations to that lifting force, which expands and rises as the day warms. Thermals are created when the day's sunlight and heat are absorbed into receptive ground, typically sloped, south-facing and bare, like the rocky, un-timbered, sage-covered hillside we were on.

Sandhill crane. Photo courtesy of Damon West Photography.

The birds must exhaust themselves propelling those heavy crane bodies the long miles from Oregon, California and points south to swamp and grassland edges somewhere up in northern BC, Arctic Canada, Alaska, even eastern Siberia. It is a measure of their evolved intelligence and memory of places that cranes have come to know, master and predict the energy-saving advantage of rising thermal air; they can gain a degree of rest, reduced air pressure, favourable tailwinds and a vaster view of the earth.

In thin sunlight, the mountains and sky to the west and southwest fade into each other like smoke. What sun there is reflects momentarily from breasts and wing and back feathers as the cranes continue their slow, nuanced turning and ascending. Body by body, their fronts and backs shift, alternately, from direct sunlight to shadow, light to dark to light and dark again. The impression is of a shifting spiral, a great auger slow-turning skyward, and opaque slow-motion winks of pale grey and tawny off-brown, wispy, muted shades, like those light-filled sky and sea paintings by the great English master J.M.W. Turner, only frameless and curving off into the void.

Marne has photos she took with her telephoto lens of the cranes in their hundreds wheeling above us in that near-colourless sky. Examining her pictures later, she said the cranes, gathering into that massive gyre up there, remind her of iron filings slowly and uniformly lining up in a three-dimensional, moving, magnetic field, coming into unison with it and each other and the far world beneath them. Sandhill cranes, and Marne the viewer and vehicle, whose actions and profound comprehension give us a passing vision of unity, a quick immersion once again into here-and-now myth time, where animals, rooted simply and absolutely in their own true natures, inform and merge with humans: Distant Time, where one plus one plus thousands equals one.

> *And that bugling sound rising, behind us, above us, coming up the valley to us; cranes conversing.*

And that bugling sound rising, behind us, above us, coming up the valley to us; cranes conversing: a babble, a gabble, a collectivity, an intention, an intelligence, an upwelling, an ascension of cranes, ethereal, boundless, wild: the suchness of sandhill cranes.

When they are gone we are gone.

After most of an hour, the size and number of vees of flying cranes tailed off somewhat abruptly. Soon there were only stragglers, a few small vees: the weak, the very young, the sick, the aged, the slow-going, the tardy. But they still talk, still encourage and advise each other, checking out the offspring, reassuring the leaders. Then there were only ones and twos and threes, then none, the last bird spirals into space. We strained to hear the last distant, sporadic crane honks, coming from somewhere up there far above us. And then there was only sky, a pale milky blue, and silence, but for those few small brown birds low in the thickets behind us, faintly chirping and twittering and living their small, busy, brown bird lives.

Later, when we drove up Mount Kobau to the south and east, as far as the snowdrifts would let us, we saw a few more stragglers, an occasional small vee, groups of two or three, following far behind and a bit to the east of the others.

Who knows how long the cranes had been coming? They were up there high above the river, basin and hillside before we arrived to hear and see them. How many eons have we been listening for and hearing those ancient voices?

There is an old story about crane stragglers passed on to us by James Teit. It involves a young Secwepemc man from up north in the mid-Fraser River area who, feeling mistreated by his home people, wanders south far beyond the Columbia River, likely passing through the Similkameen Valley as he goes. Eventually he comes to the land of the Sa'tuen, the sandhill crane people, probably a place crane flocks winter in nowadays, where he befriends an old crane man and his granddaughter. It turns out they know his homeland; they fly over it every year on their way north. They even stop in the area around Horse Lake in the Cariboo to rest. The Secwepemc man and the young woman marry, and in the spring his new crane people relatives ask him to blow crane bone whistles, put on crane feather clothes like them, and practise flying, in preparation for going north with them and all the other crane people. Each crane donates a feather from its body and a feather from its wings to assist him to fly. The granddaughter and grandfather are especially helpful with his preparation and practice, the young woman painstakingly sewing all those feathers into a crane cloak for him. Because of his limitations as a newly fledged crane person, the trio flies slowly together behind the others. This is the reason you always see a few cranes in these times, flying behind all the rest. The man continued to stay with the crane people who had welcomed him so, and he and his wife had many children.

That stretched-wire-like honking of cranes, usually from a long way off, has always stirred my blood, made me stop, twist my neck and peer, strain my eyes till they hurt, made me on occasion literally chase through the woods and along meadow and swamp edges to catch a glimpse of the sound source.

I have heard and seen them in small numbers over the years up and down the mid-Fraser River region and in the sloughs and parklands of the East Chilcotin. The Interior flyway is minor compared to the great prairie courses from Texas and Nebraska north to the boreal forests and Arctic tundra and back. Sandhill cranes do nest in central BC, and I have witnessed a pair on an island in a buggy little swamp downstream from Big Bar Lake, the female hunched into her nest in an attempt to look flat and invisible, her bright eye unmoving; the male nearby, not too close, erect, vigilant and very evidently there. We tiptoed by.

At Stack Valley above Riske Creek, not far south of Eric and Lillian Collier's preserved cabin on Meldrum Creek, I watched a courting trio—two males and a female, I presume—do a measured stalk and dance. They do a stately ritual gavotte, up from the side of a small grassland pond to the tree edge and down again, up and back, up and back, full of intention, over and over, until one—I'm assuming one of the males—can take it no more and flies away. The remaining pair stand by the pond edge, side by side, calling and calling, urgent, sad-sounding, entreating him to return, perhaps. After a little, from the far side of a strip of dark spruce timber across the pond, the departed one responds: echoey, forlorn-seeming, resigned.

In June of 2000, at Hutch Meadow below Fletcher Lake on Minton Creek, Peter Stein and I stood mesmerized as a pair of sandhill cranes, the female in front, I do believe, the male not far behind, flew in long, elegant ellipses over and around us. They were both honking in rhythmic sequence, first one, then the other, one, then the other, one, then the other, increasing the syncopation as they flew: some kind of statement of their bond together, we felt. The experience was gripping. We had disturbed them doing a stalk together on an open, shrubby slope—our intrusion, it seems, triggering the ritual mode to shift from ground to aerial. They flew over us for many minutes.

And I experienced something similar, though more momentary and not so near, with a pair of cranes at Graveyard Springs south of Tatla Lake. Only here they were being deliberately covert, especially the male, exhibiting decoy tactics so the female could retreat unseen to her nest somewhere out in the middle of the swamp. What was clear above all was the devotion of the couple for each other and their need to do whatever was necessary for the female to sit on her eggs undetected and undisturbed.

It is said cranes mate for life. Round the world they are revered for that, as well as for their mating dances, their haunting calls, their longevity, their long and arduous migrations, and, in the case of species that winter on the Indian subcontinent, their ability to fly at great elevations in extreme cold over the high Himalayas, mightiest of the world's mountain ranges. And, naturally, they are revered for their beauty. One species, the sarus, is a holy messenger of Vishnu, the Hindu deity, and is seen as a symbol of virtue and protected accordingly. As with most long-lived animal species, cranes are perceived as wise. Buddhists in Tibet, Nepal and Bhutan see cranes as vehicles of the sacred and not to be harmed.

The Ainu, aboriginals of northern Japan, and nearly gone now,

A pair of sandhill cranes. Photo courtesy of Damon West Photography.

view the red-crowned crane as both the symbol of eternal life and a messenger of death. To them, white cranes are "the marsh gods." Red crowns have the most elaborate courtship dance among cranes, and the Ainu, like many aboriginal peoples in wild crane regions, developed ritual crane dances in acknowledgment and imitation, and to be connected with the animals in spirit. In North America, various native cultures—the Ojibwa, Cree, Tlingit and others—revere cranes; in the Southwest, among the Zuni- and Tewa-speaking pueblos, there are crane clans. The Koyukon, Dene hunters of northern Alaska, hunted cranes for meat on occasion, but respected and admired them also, for their friendly support in Distant Time and for the harsh beauty of their calling.

The American naturalist Peter Matthiessen hears that crane voice for a certainty. He is a lifelong devotee of all wild nature, inner and outer, and it seems the crane species of the world hold a special awe for him, if I read his book *The Birds of Heaven* correctly. He describes an ascension of sandhill cranes: "Soon after the sun fires the horizon, the crane armies rise in stupendous celebration...It felt like they had ripped my heart out and taken it with them." He likens the experience to an earlier time when thousands of Canada geese rose close to him "in a mighty yelping roar around my ears... an exaltation of life never matched until this dawn when the sandhills rose in thunder, swirling and climbing and parting into wisps and strands of the fiery suffusion of the sunrise."

In this fine book, one of his many, Matthiessen describes in rich detail his considerable experience with, and observations of, all fifteen species of cranes on earth, most of which are in survival difficulties, some severe. The outstanding exceptions are the sandhill cranes of North America, a great recovery success, and the Eurasian cranes of Europe and western Asia. He is moved as he notes that the crane "is the most ancient of all birds, the oldest living bird species."

Closer to our own land, Harry Robinson, Okanagan elder and storyteller, who lived upriver near Hedley, and who died fairly recently, recounted to Wendy Wickwire a nearly endless series of stories and myth-stories from the Okanagan area, detail by detail. One in particular was about two hunters from up north who received a gift of power, a perpetual food supply, from two tall sandhill crane people who were camped with their crane friends close by. The condition was that the hunters should keep quiet about the source. Of course, one blabbed to his wife, who spread the story far and wide, and the supernatural food source disappeared instantaneously. So it's clear: cranes have power, and discretionary silence is a virtue.

Over tens of thousands of years, our hunting and gathering and early agriculturist ancestors experienced all elements of nature as animate, endowed with life or spirit, the world of dreams no less than the material world. Most elements, outer or inner, merited the fullest possible attention for signs of portent, especially in the ongoing hunt of animals for meat. Any significant encounters, such as the rising majesty of several thousand sandhill cranes on a cool spring morning or a sharp-edged night-time dream containing possibilities for meaning, transformation and survival, are grounds for careful scrutiny and response. In that old, shamanistic realm of light sky, land, dark underground places and dreaming, spanning the northern hemi-sphere from Scandinavia to Siberia to Greenland, the world was perceived as much through mythic as empiric lenses. And if, in that archaic world, powerfully wild beings—owls, cranes, buffalo, bears, moose or predator cats—were featured, if in dreams their trails crossed yours, we were—and perhaps still are—bound to take serious note.

Over tens of thousands of years, our ancestors experienced all elements of nature as animate, endowed with life or spirit, the world of dreams no less than the material world.

When it comes to dreaming, I am like that unnamed Navaho man, quoted in some standard anthropology text long ago, who claimed poverty for hav-ing few dreams: I too am dream-poor, or at least I do not remember them well. Two days before our visitation with the cranes above Blind Creek and Cawston, Marne and I were travelling to the Lower Similkameen from Victoria. We had stopped for the night with her parents in Vancouver, and in that unfamiliar environment I experienced an unusually vivid and disturbing venture into living dream time.

Late in that dark night in Bob and Mary's basement bedroom, I found myself locked in protracted physical combat with a large spotted cat, likely a jaguar. This animal is a power in Mayan and Olmec mythology, capable of entering the soul and dream worlds of humans, so they say. For sure it was a fierce feline creature with bared teeth, like the vine-covered stone jaguar faces we had seen in a television documentary about Mayan outposts in the jungles of Chiapas in southern Mexico earlier in the week. I felt no fear and was able to ward it off for a time, but I became exhausted, "mortally, mortally tired," in the precise words in my mind's ear in dream time. Eventually, as we engaged in deadly struggle at the top of a small shaded rock face or parapet, the animal knocked me off onto the forest floor below. The ground cover around was dry low bush in open coniferous woods; that is where the beast got me.

I came to partially buried and helpless, with dirt scuffed over me, the way cats do when they half-bury their prey, in the dark, on the damp earth floor of a stone under-room or small cave at the base of the rock face. Narrow shafts of bright light shone through holes and slits in a semi-wall of stacked stones. I was attempting, over and over, to call out, to speak, to connect with others, anybody, but was unable, utterly, to make the slightest sound. It was terribly frustrating to be so completely and finally silent.

I awoke from the jaguar encounter feeling exposed and at risk. I've had the sense for some time that our culture is disconnecting, most notably between the powerfully rich and the poor, but in many small ways between us all; the concept of the common good is largely gone, and the values of empathy and trust seem too often to be beyond our comprehension and capacity to experience. The liveliness and integrity of wild nature, inner and outer, is mainly unnoticed, and more and more the old connecting notions of spirit and "soul" are inconceivable, even laughable to some. Such narrowing restricts creativity and well-being, and impedes possibilities. I came away from that dream with the conviction that, in this era of forgetting, where most elements of nature are rendered inert, I must try to defend the fragility of our inner, subtle world where I can.

Two days later, standing and gazing up at cranes with Marne at Blind Creek, experiencing those great birds in their thousands rising and spiralling in the sky, I felt the dolorous effects of the jaguar dream fade. Darkness was supplanted by light. Balance and my sense of the liveliness of things returned. I was grateful, but my commitment to be mindful of vulnerabilities in a hardening world remains.

That which is most subtle is most powerful. Love abides.

LOVE AND FAITH IN CHOPAKA

Fear is the frightened child.
Love is the flame of holy remembering.
     —Pat Rodegast and Judith Stanton

DOWNRIVER AT CHOPAKA, ON THE SAME DAY AS THE GREAT SPIRALLING ascension of cranes in their thousands above Blind Creek, Casey Sanders and an elderly bachelor friend and neighbour named Charley Horse Squakin were standing outside on the road, taking in the pleasant spring morning and talking. In a quiet moment they heard the gabble of cranes, looked up to see if they could spot the great birds making their way north and, after some peering, exclaimed at their numbers high in the sky above the Lower Similkameen River valley. Casey says that people don't usually notice the cranes passing, and it is an event when they do hear and see them. Perhaps, like most migrating birds, sandhill cranes choose sometimes to fly at night.

Charley Horse, who had lived in the small house across the road from Casey and his wife, Lillian Allison, died only a few years ago. Charley was something of a healer and had helped Lillian with some of her long-term injury and health issues. He used to gather and prepare bitterroot (speet-lum) and other herbs and would give some to Lillian to use; they'd talk plants and the practice of Indian medicine together. She showed Marne and me some speetlum that she and Casey had gathered and readied themselves

Our Lady of Lourdes church at Chopaka in the Lower Similkameen. Photo courtesy of Marne St. Claire.

and kept in their freezer; it has the colour and look of fine vermicelli.

Lillian and Casey live a short distance up the road from Our Lady of Lourdes, the Roman Catholic church at Chopaka, and the big cemetery close to it. The church, a small, simply built, century-old building with a fresh coat of paint, stands firmly at the edge of a grove of red-trunked ponderosa pines. A few old, shadowed log houses sit empty in the young woods behind. The large, well-peopled cemetery is across and down the road, and there is a little old ranch and one or two homes beyond that; the entire congregation of buildings is immediately north of the US border. In open places up the slope behind the church, late-spring patches of golden balsamroot sunflowers glow like low shafts of sunlight through the trees. Nearby, Nehumpchin (nxum m'cin) Creek roars down off Snowy Mountain in a hurry to reach the big river on the bottom side of the hayfields, sloughs and cottonwood flats.

Lillian and Casey are confirmed practitioners of the Roman Catholic faith and are elders and lay ministers in their church, but they are open to the old spiritual values also. Lillian is First Nations; Casey is from Holland. On Sundays, before the monthly service, he rises early and walks down to the church to turn up the heat. In older times, before electricity, a fire would have been kindled in the woodstove early to be certain the building was comfortably warm. After the service, he and Lillian invite everyone over to their home for an open house and lunch, much as her grandmother and mother had done, so many years before. When Lillian was more mobile, the couple went down to the cemetery frequently to visit the grave of Lillian's mother, Mary, a profound figure in both their lives, and they are sure she continues to be there with them now. They talk with her, ask her for guidance and listen quietly for answers. They ask "What would Mom do?" And the responses they receive always seem to work. Lillian's rancher father, Bobby Allison, a kind and gentle, hard-working man, and also a pivotal person in Lillian's life, is buried there not far away. Both he and Lillian's brother, Bert, died at a relatively young age: her father was fifty-four, her brother only forty-two. Mary Allison died at age seventy-seven.

Formerly, Lillian and Casey had operated Brushy Bottom, a bed and breakfast, off the Chopaka road and down a narrow driveway on the same lower side as the hayfields, the feeding Canada geese and the winding Similkameen. The welcome sign engraved in Okanagan, S ntuxt,' means "you're going [crawling] through the bushes." Their home, hidden from the road by thick willows and white birches, is nonetheless open and full of light in its small clearing; it is a modest, immaculate place, neat as a pin, snug as a bug. The garden is similarly trim, with a hummingbird feeder, spring bulbs, a tidy lawn, places to sit, and an automatic gate and watering system. Guests came to visit from all over in those B & B days. Casey was careful to mention to them that if you look south from here through an opening in the trees, you can spot the snowy-haired maiden on Chopaka Mountain (c'upaq), lying up there on that rocky ridge in repose, stretched out, staring at the sky.

Huge, glacier-worn, granite boulders are a part of their landscape. Lillian remembers that when she and her sisters and brother were young and gathered around, her mother would sit on the largest, a long and imposing thing close to where the house is now, and tell old family stories from it. During the construction of their new home, Lillian had originally hoped that the house plan could incorporate that monumental rock in some way, but that proved not to be practical. The valley is quiet, though the distant sound of Nehumpchin Creek next to Charley Horse's home is a constant. And late-afternoon breezes sigh through dry-needled conifers: yellow pine and Douglas fir.

There had been a pair of well-used sweathouses in the brush down the creek below Charley's house, but now, with his passing, they are half covered in cottonwood leaves from the previous fall, and shrubs and small trees around them are closing in, filling spaces. Charley's sister, after most of a long lifetime, moved up from San Diego to live in his old place. She and Lillian and Casey kept an eye out for each other for a few years before she too passed on. Mourning doves talk quietly back and forth in the swamp, one close, the other farther away. There is a low insistence in their calling. A pileated woodpecker calls out. The scent of balm of Gilead is in the air.

Lillian and her siblings were raised, in part, on a ranch up the road, like their parents and grandparents on their father's side before them; a log barn and young Bert's white-picket-fenced gravesite stand at the old home place now. Another portion of their parents' ranch was upriver on the far side of Keremeos at Standing Rock, and some years the family lived up there. The girls went to day schools in Cawston and Keremeos, but they were educated in some of the old Indian ways as well. When Lillian, and now Casey, hear or see something unusual in the animal world, like a small bird hitting a window, or a great horned owl at night, fluttering and flapping on the windshield of their car, they stop to acknowledge and comprehend the incident. They know that birds bring messages, sometimes of death, and it takes a quiet heart and mind to hear them. They offer prayers for healing and safety, and understanding.

Several times over the years, Marne and I visited Brushy Bottom on the Easter weekend in spring, and it has been our pleasure to come to know, respect and care for Lillian and Casey. Marne and I go for walks and short drives, enjoying the time of year, spring birds and the slow-moving river as we do so, and later we talk with Lillian and Casey about life, history and spiritual matters. The Chopaka Rodeo falls on that same Easter weekend each year, and horse folks from all over the Okanagan, Nicola and Similkameen areas, and

Chopaka Rodeo. Photo courtesy of Marne St. Claire.

from down in the States, gather to let winter go for another year. They socialize, enjoy the setting, test their horses and watch good riders variously ride or fall off large, frequently resistant and not particularly domestic roughstock.

We dropped in to the rodeo from time to time. It is held up the road a way on a beautiful little flat on the downhill side, with views of the valley and mountains all around. The weather is usually glorious. There is nothing like an early spring day in the Lower Similkameen; the air is clear and warm, with maybe a touch of high-country cool coming down off the snow-covered slopes and peaks above us if the breezes shift. There are trucks and stock trailers parked, horses cavorting and meeting new horses, birds flitting, kids playing, having fun. People are gathered around the back ends of pickup boxes in groups, talking, catching up, eating fry bread or hamburgers, or out walking their horses, showing off, calling out. The announcer is up in the booth informing the assembled multitude of the next event—where the rider hails from, the name of the horse he or she is riding—and the fact that Marty's left his lights on, and could Dorothy or Gramma Doreen go and collect their grandkid, "he's looking kind of lost." There are some rangy bovine critters with a Texas longhorn look and a glint in their eye in a pen next to the rodeo ring, edging out in hopes of reaching open country. The speaker suggests with the same flat-voiced composure, but with an added hint of urgency, that "You boys better get over there and close that gate, eh? That stock is gonna go wild on us." He has an easy, relaxed voice with just the right twang and drawl and is on first-name, talking terms with everybody here it seems; he's done this job for a good long while.

The leaves have turned on the poplars and cottonwoods down along the flats now, that same grey-greenish wispy tinge as happens up in the Cariboo–Chilcotin, only weeks earlier down here on the border; the leaves are not even out upriver at Princeton yet. But Lillian has already seen signs of her favourite of all spring sightings, sage buttercups on the road edges. She usually spies them first at a certain place not far from her brother Bert's gravesite.

She and Casey, and the congregation, meanwhile, will have been to the church service and had Holy Communion; they will have returned to Brushy Bottom and be setting things up for lunch. Lillian Allison will be walking slow and steady in that measured, careful walk of hers. She walks about the kitchen, into the dining area, carrying a plate of cold cuts and cheese maybe, bowls of soup or a handful of cutlery, the sound of her footsteps hard and solid, a slow marching rhythm, a low beat with unstoppable intention on her vacuumed-this-morning floor. The room is tidy and shiny, like the gleaming "no-water" pot set for healthy cooking that Lillian is so proud of. "There isn't a pot you can't find a lid for," she states, as if she'd heard and said those words before. That saying comes from her mother, Mary. Lillian believes that, knowing her dear daughter was getting on in age, disabled and without a mate, Mary would utter the statement from time to time as a way of saying "Don't give up."

Lillian, you see, has been in two major automobile accidents, the first in 1965 when she was young, alone and perhaps not paying enough attention ("perhaps foolish" as Lillian puts it) and her car went off the highway. As well, she was a passenger in a second car accident in 1982. These events left her severely wounded and disabled, with twice-broken back, broken neck, shattered legs and feet and kneecap, lesions, extreme pain, and scars over her body to show for it all. The inevitably severe pain she experienced throughout her body left her in despair at times, but never completely helpless. She had strength and stamina, faith, will, intelligence, a supportive family, modern medical technology and a high pain threshold.

Lillian had to learn to lock her knee—the one without a kneecap— as she moved, and with every step she took, with each move she made, from before she rose from the bed in the morning to her preparation for rest and sleep at night, Lillian paid full, acute attention as thoroughly and for as long as she was capable. For if she did not, if she lost the acuity of her concentration, her seeing and feeling, from distraction or fatigue or a momentary lapse, if she became careless and made an error of motion, she

Lillian Allison as a young woman. Photo courtesy of Lillian Allison.

risked doing major damage to herself. She risked undoing the decades of pain, medical intervention, courage, practice, healing and care that had been essential to her arrival here in this low-built, wheelchair-ready, ground-level home with Casey, her partner at Chopaka.

That Lillian was walking at all is astonishing, another of life's many true miracles. That series of small, steady, almost drum-like thumps we became accustomed to hearing was the sound of her specially constructed shoes with the built-in artificial heels as she makes her patient way about the house. I can hear and picture Lillian walking from the kitchen into their fine front living room, with the east-facing windows and the morning sunlight flooding in. She is silent, her face serious and intent as she moves. The room is baroque with aboriginal art and mementos, paintings, antique lamps, Delft porcelains and Dutch memorabilia carefully and judiciously placed, and the large, three-dimensional eagle over the fireplace, the cross of Jesus on the wall.

Lillian walked in that steadfastly determined manner as if she could and would walk that way forever. "I have learned to live with pain quite well, and can tolerate a lot and, of course, hide it," she told Marne and me at one point, her face momentarily grim. "No use complaining; what good would that do? They can't do anything for me. I've lived with continual pain for over forty years; I don't know what normal is anyway."

Initially told she would never walk, Lillian has had a total of eighty-five corrective surgeries so far and has spent eight and a half years of her life in hospitals and rehabilitation units. Many of her surgeries were long and complicated: she underwent skin grafts, dozens of invasions to her body and soul, dozens of bouts of anesthesia, over years and years, so that she could be rebuilt and healed as much as the limits of modern medicine would allow. Six and a half years of that time were spent in residence at Shaughnessy Hospital for veterans in Vancouver. Now she has a plate on her leg to help keep it intact. And through it all she carries a demeanour of calm and discipline and focus. "I've brushed close to death so many times; I even died for four minutes at one time," she says. Those lost moments necessitated a year of hard rehab for her to regain her mental acuity. "I've learned to live each day, each living breath, as if it were my last." Lillian has a deep, lifelong personal practice in the Divine, and a long relationship of love, devotion, shared faith and delight with Casey, her husband, constant partner and support.

"Enjoy life, but be careful; don't waste it away for nothing. Life is too short to be fighting."

"Enjoy life," she advises, "but be careful; don't waste it away for nothing. Life is too short to be fighting. You need to take the time to smell the roses." Now, after all those difficult years, Lillian is a person who likes to laugh, whose smiling, laughing face glows like a warm summer's morning.

Certainly her life is about love unconditional. In those early years, when her physical destruction was most critical and overwhelming, Lillian had her family: her father, her sisters, relatives, friends and above all else, but for the Creator, her mother, Mary, to look after her. Here, beyond even the wonder of her physical recovery, is where Lillian's story is most clearly remarkable. Mary, with her years of love and faith and hard work; and, more latterly, Casey, with his strength and devotion; and Lillian herself, of course, were determined that she would survive, heal and live a good life. Mary's fundamental counsel to her daughter always was "patience, have patience." She advised her Lilly to save herself for marriage. "No one wants a second hand." A loving mother's heart transcends and transforms.

Mary would do the cooking, washing, housework, driving and all the other dawn-to-nightfall minutiae of daily home life, and with her husband, Bobby, she would assist Lillian up and down and in and out, accompanying her on the many visits and trips, back and forth, to government agencies, to hospitals, to doctors, to specialists, and on long car rides to and from Vancouver. And when the path of Lillian's healing began to seem reasonably secure, Mary wondered about her wounded daughter's longer future. Who would care for Lilly when she, Mary, was gone? How would she survive? Mary must surely have asked that question a thousand times.

Casey Sanders has his own story of hardship and struggle. Born in the Netherlands before the Second World War and the German occupation of his country, the stories of his young life centre on his family and their long, desperate fight to find enough to eat and to stay alive. They came out of the war intact, with instincts honed for self-preservation and, like many post-war Europeans, a desire to emigrate and make a new life, in their case, in Canada. The family found themselves in Alberta, and Casey, his brothers and his father worked in the coal mines south of Edson for several years. Casey, his parents, his brothers and their families saved up their resources and moved to Cawston, then to Keremeos. Although trained as a machinist in the old country, Casey continued to widen his range of practical skills and worked as a bus driver, mechanic and manager of a gas station and machine shop. He still owns several vintage cars. He was a man in his middle years when his wife Jeanne died.

Keremeos is a small town. Mary Allison and members of the Allison

Mary Allison, mother of Lillian. Photo courtesy of Lillian Allison.

family had known Casey personally because of his bus driving, his reputation as a skilled and steady worker, his regular attendance at church and other community functions. Mary saw qualities in his character: his values and intelligence, his trustworthiness, his work ethic, his devoted support of his wife through her illness. She saw Casey as a good man.

Lillian recounts, "It so happens that my niece Marcey worked at the local bowling alley and signed our family into a mixed league team. When the time came to bowl, the men and boys of the family decided not to. My sister Barbara said, 'Why don't you ask Casey?' Her husband, Henry, worked for Casey driving school bus. 'He's alone now and it would be good to get him out of the house and doing something different.' So that is how Casey got involved with our family.

"Of course, Mom was in her glory. She and Casey got along fabulously, and to her, he could do no wrong. She saw potential there for her Lilly. She would encourage me to sit closer to him at the bowling alley, but I was shy and embarrassed and I ignored her intentions. I can only guess that she thought this could be a good match, made in heaven. Mom saw Casey not only as a good husband but as a full-time caregiver as well.

"He called me late one night to say that something was really bothering him. With me being a Jehovah's Witness at the time and him a Catholic, Casey believed our thoughts of marriage were not going to work. He said that he would not give me much choice—he was falling in love, and if I wanted to remain a Witness it would be better to end it now. I cried and cried. We ended our conversation, and I could not sleep."

The next day, Casey told his mother what he had done. She bawled him out and told him that if he lost that girl he would have no one to blame but himself. She said he should go and apologize to Mary for what he had done to her and to Lilly.

Casey went to Mary's home after work that same day and related to her what he had said to Lillian; expecting an earful, he apologized. She told him, "Stand up now." Casey thought she was going to hit him—instead she cried and hugged him like he had never been hugged before, saying, "Thank you, thank you. I have prayed for eighteen years for my Lilly to come home, and now the Creator has sent me help. My prayers have finally been answered."

Casey told Lillian he was very sorry for what happened. He said that he had been thinking and had come up with a solution that he thought might clear things up. He said, "If you change your religion and I change mine, we can go down the middle of the road together." Lillian did not agree to that, and told him, "No. If anyone's going to change, I'll change mine." She was aware that Casey was a devout Roman Catholic, as was his whole family, and she knew that her mother, Mary, had been praying for many years that her Lillian would "come home" to the Catholic religion.

In a talk later with Mary, Casey said that he loved her daughter and asked if he could give Lillian a ring. Mary responded yes, but after her initial excitement she said, "Lillian is an adult. She can make up her own mind to say yes or no." She reminded him that "in our tradition, once a couple gets married, the man becomes the boss and the wife is to obey the husband." Casey said he did not agree with that way; in his eyes, "neither is the boss."

In Lillian's own words: "The next afternoon [January 29], Casey came to the house. As I was coming out of the bedroom, he stopped me and said 'Here' and handed me the engagement ring. Then he turned and walked back into the dining room. I followed him and held my hand up to show my ring to Mom. She and I both started to cry, then I showed my sister Anne and we all cried together. Even our friend Connie started crying. Casey asked, 'What have I done? Why are you crying?' We all said, 'No no, you've done nothing wrong. These are tears of happiness and joy for both of us.' Someone said, 'We never thought Lillian would get engaged or married. Lillian's always been so fussy all her life.' After they all stopped crying, Mary sat herself down in her easy chair and called up her best friend, Betty Terbasket. When she started talking, the first words out of her mouth were, 'Guess what, I've got the bestest news in the whole world to tell you. It's January 29 and 15 minutes past 1 PM and my Lilly just got engaged!' Then they and all the rest of us started crying again."

In August 1989, Lillian and Casey married. Two and a half months later, Mary spoke to Lillian. She said "I can see that you are happy, so I can go now." Two weeks following, Mary Allison had a massive stroke and died, her life task completed. On Mary's carved, wooden grave marker in the community cemetery, near Bobby's grave, below her name and dates are the words "Proverbs 31: 10–31." The verses are a detailed, Old Testament description of a woman of service, beginning with "Who can find a virtuous woman? For her price is far above rubies."

Down the fence line from the Allison graves, Charley Horse Squakin is buried. His grave mound is bright with plastic flowers and a rooster with a whirligig tail. The headboard is new and shiny and, like many of the more recent grave markers, made from wood. Charley's day of dying is indicated— "Closing Time March 3—2004"—and his motto, "Easy Does it," is inscribed below that; Charley hadn't touched liquor in years. On the back there is a heart, and in it the neatly carved words "Charley + Dolly." That's Dolly Parton we're talking about here.

Charley the healer had played a role in Lillian's path to improved health, especially in one instance when she had a deep lesion that would not heal. He was persistent, and when he noticed that she was given to drinking quantities of diet Coke, he exclaimed with some frustration, "I can do all the praying, and praying in my sweathouse, and using all the Indian medicines and all the whiteman's medicines to help heal you. But as long as you keep drinking that damn pop, you're never going to heal." She quit Coca Cola, he continued his treatment and in two weeks the lesion was gone.

Lillian and Casey live a modest, grateful, happy life together. They serve not only the church and each other, but their larger community as well. Lillian

Lillian and Casey on their wedding day, August 26, 1989. Photo courtesy of Lillian Allison and Casey Sanders.

has been an active, long-term member and advocate on executives, boards and advisory counsels of many province-wide support organizations, including the BC Aboriginal Network on Disability Society (BCANDS), and has stories to tell of her travels and experiences. Her curriculum vitae is a long one. Casey is entirely devoted to assisting Lillian: driving and accompanying her to the many meetings and conferences she attends, making sure her life is secure and, at all times, helping her to get about physically. He does most of the basic maintenance and backup at Brushy Bottom. Casey is on call to help all hours of the day and night. How many of us are sufficiently strong of soul and heart and body to serve with such constant dedication?

Lillian still cooks and serves good meals. When we have visited, before we begin to eat, she says an inclusive grace, beginning in sibilant Okanagan and concluding in English, with abundant personal references to guests and

Grave at Chopaka Cemetery. Photo courtesy of Marne St. Claire.

others in their lives, always expressing gratitude and asking for support. We hold hands around the table and, hearts light, share our fare in the sure knowledge we are, for these moments, in grace.

One evening I asked Lillian if there were some Bible verses that have particular meaning for her. She took time to carefully search for several sets: 1 Corinthians 1: 4–8: words of thanks and confirmation to the Creator; Isaiah 35: 5–6: *Then the eyes of the blind shall be opened,...the lame man leap...*; the gospel of Matthew 25: 34–45: *You gave me shelter, I give you peace...*; 1 Corinthians 13: 3–13: *Love is patient and kind...*; Revelation 21: 4–5: *And God shall wipe away all tears from their eyes; ...neither shall there be any more pain...*; Psalm 25: *Unto thee, O Lord, do I lift up my soul*; and Psalm 23: *The lord is my shepherd; I shall not want...*, yet another Psalm of David.

Lillian and Casey had a collection of exceptionally well-crafted Okanagan and Nlaka'pamux (Thompson) Indian baskets. Several of the best examples are on show at the Mascot Mines tour centre in Hedley. Displayed in Lillian and Casey's living room was more fine basketry; they have as well some of the most remarkable tanned deerskin and beading imaginable, including a marvellous dress, all of it the outcome of hours of concentrated preparation and years of skilled practice. The quality of the tanning, the uniformly pale colour, the thick softness and pliability of the hide, are all flawless. The dress was made by a well-known craftswoman from the Sse'lictcen (Flathead) Nation in western Montana. On our last visit, Lillian insisted Marne try it on. Marne was honoured. Lillian said, with her smile, "We are all family now."

In Lillian and Casey's house are old, framed family photos with a sepia tinge, reminders of where they live and who they are connected to. One, hanging in the bedroom where we sleep, is of Lillian's grandparents, Selina and Neil Bent, with their children around them, in front of a substantial, squared-log house. Lillian's mother, Mary, an infant in a small cradleboard, is balanced against Selina's knees in front and, head turned sharply, is looking up most pointedly at her father, obviously, in that moment, fascinated by him. He is standing tall and wearing an old-style, flat-brimmed campaign hat, like a Mountie hat, with the four same-sized dints, one for each quarter of the crown, much in vogue at the turn of the twentieth century. Neil's brim is as flat as a hat brim can be. Mary's older, taller brother is beside, and her older sister is standing behind on a high chair; their mother has a worried look. The house has well-notched corners. It stood down at the bottom of the Chopaka road, south of the church, where the little old ranch beyond the cemetery is situated now.

Lillian and her sisters can trace their many relatives throughout the Similkameen, Okanagan and Merritt regions of southern British Columbia and beyond. Among their various forebears is John Fall Allison, the first significant European settler at Princeton in the early 1860s. He was one of the first cattle ranchers in southern BC and is the Allison sisters' great-grandfather. In 1860, having informed Governor James Douglas of the existence of a pass through the Cascade Mountains, Allison was authorized to clear a trail forthwith to Vermilion Forks (later renamed Princeton). Now called Allison Pass, it is situated south of the two high routes that became known as the Dewdney and Hope Pass Trails, and is the route of the current

Hope–Princeton highway. Later in 1860, John Fall Allison was contracted by Douglas to open several more trails in the region.

Like most non-native trailblazers, Allison followed long-established Indian trails; in fact, his first wife, Nora (Xilxatkw), was a horse packer and entrepreneur in her own right, and had her own forty-horse pack train. She knew and used some of those old trails to and from the mine workings at Rock Creek, east of the Okanagan Valley, as part of her own business, and undoubtedly showed them, and the Allison Pass route as well, to her country partner. Nora and John had three children; one, Bertie, was grandfather to Lillian and her sisters.

John Fall Allison is buried in a small private cemetery above his Princeton ranch site, below Castle Rock on the front edge of Miner Mountain; his second wife, Susan, Scottish and mother of fourteen children, lies next to him. John and Susan were married in 1868. After raising all those sons and daughters, surviving various disasters with equanimity and managing the family enterprises in John Fall's frequent, work-related absences, Susan wrote her invaluable *Recollections of a Pioneer of the Sixties*, a Western Canadian classic, later edited, notated, retitled (*A Pioneer Gentlewoman in British Columbia*) and published by noted historian Margaret Ormsby.

Mr. Allison was ancestor to many descendants, aboriginal and white, and some still live in the Similkameen Valley. His great-granddaughter Linda Allison, from Susan's side of the family, operates Allison Creek Ranch on her own today. Lillian's oldest sister, Barbara, was recently chief of the Lower Similkameen First Nations band; another sister, Bernie, was employed in Ottawa at the time we first met her and, as a self-professed lover of education, was learning the Punjabi language; then there is the indomitable Anne, grandmother of Darius and young Morgan, two fine lads in their own right, who manages a business in Penticton; and lastly there is Ramona, the third oldest, who is, in Lillian's words, "energetic, outgoing, full of hell and vinegar and a flirt." She too has her own business. Over the years there have been family reunions reacquainting the various members with each other. Each of the Allison sisters takes pride in her cultural heritage from all sides of the

The Selina and Neil Bent family. Lillian's mother, Mary, is in the cradleboard, circa 1912. Photo courtesy of Lillian Allison.

family. They know who they are and where they came from; they acknowledge Xilxatkw and Susan Allison equally.

All five Allison sisters have ranched. When they were young, they were variously active around their parents' ranch; Anne, Bernie and brother Bert did the riding with the cattle, feeding them when they had to and driving them to spring and summer ranges over on Little Chopaka and Kruger Mountains and up by Hedley. Everybody helped out with the farm chores: moving irrigation pipe, haying, working the kitchen garden, and the myriad other duties involved in maintaining a lively farm business. Those who weren't working outside helped Mary with the cooking and housework. Much of the work was done early, before school, and after they returned home at night. There wasn't much time for play. Lillian says that in her later years she helped her mom "where she could."

Once, after Marne and I had walked partway up an old, steep, logging track along nearby Susap Creek one afternoon, Lillian mentioned she'd gone up that same trail, an old route through reserve land to the high country, when she was young; her brother-in-law Henry was up there Cat-logging. She remembered that little trip as special. I'd been talking earlier with her sister Anne, for whom those old stock trails and childhood trips were also memorable, and who obviously had revelled in the ranch life of those times. I asked her, knowing the answer already, if she missed the old-time horse world.

"Every day," she said, giving me and the wall a faraway look.

TIME PASSES AND THE WINDS OF CHANGE HAVE BLOWN THROUGH LITTLE Chopaka. Life events, including catastrophic ones, inevitably occur. Sadly, there is a profoundly radical sequel to Lillian and Casey's story, originally written in 2006.

The tragic truth is that now Lillian can no longer walk. She is paralyzed from her waist down. On July 21, 2007, after midnight, she experienced a fall in their bathroom: she felt herself losing balance and tried to grab a railing but fell hard, hitting her back against the edge of the bathtub. Her body went cold from the shock. She was shaking and having trouble breathing, and her pain was so "excruciating" that later, about 4:30 AM, Casey drove Lillian to the emergency ward at the Penticton Hospital. Their wait was a long one. Having had her back broken twice in her two car accidents, she was sure from the start that she had broken it again. The symptoms were all the same.

Over the next four months, their efforts to get a thorough physical examination, an accurate diagnosis and, hopefully, some kind of remedy and relief for Lillian were frustrating and slow. After what seemed like a perfunctory examination, her family physician told them, "Everything looks okay." Lillian did receive medication for the chronic pain, and the dosage was increased several times. She and Casey made many visits, more than one a week on average, to various doctors in the south Okanagan; over time she got bone scans, chest and thoracic spine x-rays and, in late November, confirmation that her back was indeed broken once again. At least at that time, Lillian was still able to walk.

On December 23 of that same year, at home, as she moved to stand up, Lillian "felt something shift" in her back and found immediately, to her great dismay, that she could not move her lower body and legs. The following March she was admitted to Vancouver General Hospital under the care and direction of a spine specialist. Four days later she underwent eleven hours of back surgery—she would have four more major operations, as well as several minor ones to rectify deep bedsores. Then Lillian was referred to the G.F. Strong Rehabilitation Centre, where she remained hospitalized for more than seventeen months (including her prior stay at VGH). She was, of course, feeling hugely discouraged.

The spine specialist was moved to inform Lillian's family doctor that if she had come under his care before Christmas, "she'd still be walking." Lillian was told that she had the right to sue, but she replied, "No, that would not make me walk again."

Casey stayed in various places in Vancouver to be with her. Their financial burden was heavy, and once in a while he slept in their car in the Rehab Centre parking lot. He would rise early, avail himself of the hospital washrooms and cafeteria, and spend the day from dawn to bedtime, as he did every day, month after month, looking after Lillian. When he made an occasional short trip back to Chopaka to deal with home issues, she missed him powerfully; staff described her as a "total basket case." The couple's friendliness and hand-in-hand devotion to each other was noted throughout the hospital. Soon Casey was helping provide convalescent and, as a lay minister, spiritual care and inspiration (including "reading the rosary"), for other patients as well. Before Casey and Lillian finally returned to Chopaka, Centre staff, including doctors, gratefully awarded Casey an "honorary doctor's degree" and an inscribed stethoscope for his services.

Home again, they continue to face obstacles, many of them financial. As they live on reserve land, they are unable to get a mortgage on their house to pay for the automated wheelchair that Lillian needs and the conversion of their new van to wheelchair access. This latter involves the installation of an elevator, a difficult and expensive job. It was necessary for Casey, who was seventy-nine then, to drive the van across the American plains in November weather to far-off Minneapolis–St. Paul in Minnesota so the job could be done. Including the return flight home, the trip took two and a half days. In December 2011, Casey and Lillian flew together to Minneapolis to drive the van back to BC. They were able to sell most of their Indian basket collection and, as well, were fortunate to receive an unexpected and substantial donation from a fellow parishioner in Osoyoos to help them out. "I feel I can go for another ten to fifteen years, and I just hope I can do it with Lillian," Casey tells me.

I state my awe at Lillian's unflagging calm and graciousness; Casey agrees. "I could not imagine a better woman," he whispers as Lillian whistles a blithe tune in a nearby room. "She's never once been mad at me, not once. We go to sleep holding hands." To limit the effects of bedsores and lesions, Casey needs to turn Lillian's body over several times each night. He sets his alarm and rises every two or three hours to do so, night after night. He looks at me and says quietly, "I'm going to look after Lily till the day I die." There is no hint of self-pity in his voice. "I don't know what I'd do if I was paralyzed."

We are discussing the general shortage of wheelchair ramps, especially in rural places. "We're like prisoners here," Casey states, "our life is lonely." Social support from their community has been mixed. "We sit in the mall in Penticton sometimes and watch people," he tells me. "I hold Lily's hand. Once a lady came up to us and asked, 'Are you from Keremeos?' We replied that we were, and she said, 'I've heard about you. I was told about your love for each other.'"

Lillian in her mobile chair, her strong face glowing like a late-spring sunflower, joins Casey and me at the kitchen table as we talk; in the good morning light you notice the smoothness of her skin. We are drinking cups of hot, steeped "x x m p," "Indian" tea. I ask her what she thinks of married life. "It was the best thing I ever did," she replies, "but I was scared at first." Outside the windows, small birds of several species, including the year's first hummingbirds, mainly rufous, are clustered around feeders, and woodpeckers knock in the birches.

Now, above where binoculars and a bird book used to be, there are sheets of paper taped to windowpanes, curtains, walls, the backs of chairs, anything, with lists of words and phrases in the Okanagan language hand-printed in red, and their translations to English in blue. Lillian and her sisters are working to improve their facility with their mother tongue, a long-range project. She comments that she is able to learn meanings and sentence structure well enough but struggles with the pronunciations.

And I remind myself yet again that Lillian is in constant, often severe, pain, day and night. "The pain down my side and leg feels like I'm on fire," she says in a matter-of-fact way, and smiles as if there is nothing too wrong with that. She works out with wrist weights in hopes of gaining strength and some small recovery, and notes that she feels life in one of her legs. "It kicks a little," she says.

There is an air of strength and refinement about Lillian that is unwavering. Her fine-honed awareness of life seems to emanate from a place within her that is greater than her personal sense of self and deeper than the transient surfaces of things. For Marne the words "dignity," "nobility" and "precision" most accurately apply. No doubt these qualities are all an outcome of her early desperation and need to find the courage and perseverance it takes to learn to transcend pain and fear; for sure they are a consequence of a long adult life-practice—minutes and hours and days and years—of fully focused and profoundly necessary attention. I have known only a very few individuals as consistently realized and spiritually whole as Lillian Allison; I can only see her story as holy.

Lillian lives and breathes her faith. In her world, purpose and unity—and love and surrender—prevail. She states, "I get my strength from prayer," and again, as she has maintained throughout all those years of pain and disappointment, she reiterates, "Everything happens for a reason."

But as much as we laud Lillian for her quiet, hard-won liberation and personal authority, we must wonder equally at the totality of Casey's devotion, support and love. It is Casey's boundless dedication that allows Lillian's life to be bearable and even joyful under these most difficult of circumstances.

Lillian and Casey, spring 2012. Photo courtesy of Marne St. Claire.

And let us quietly acknowledge that it is the couple's mutual dedication to each other that enables Casey to carry on. These are exemplary people, as too was Mary Allison. Mary demonstrated each day how a life of service to others is a life well lived. These three are people who know (or knew) what love and intrinsic truth—and faith—mean.

Mary lived a modest and abstemious life. She was of that last generation where marriages were sometimes arranged, and most aboriginal folks learned as a matter of course how to use wild plants for foods, medicines and materials of various kinds. She would often go out to gather tamarack branches, bitterroot and other useful plants, and occasionally Casey would accompany her. As they walked she prayed and talked with him about how to live a good married life. "You will need patience with Lilly," Mary told him. She knew well that Lilly was slow doing her various tasks. "You could feel her sincerity," Casey says. "You could feel her strongly held wisdom. She'd talk about the ancestors, the Creator, and the importance of recognizing all things in our world as connected and in balance. It is our job to pass that knowledge on to our young children. That way, hopefully, the next generation will carry it on. That was the centre of what Mary had to say. God, could that woman pray!"

"She took nothing for granted," Casey states. "If you picked or gathered something, Mary would pray, and you had to pay for it. You must leave something: tobacco, a little money maybe—even a couple of pennies will do. But you always leave something." Lillian adds that her mother told her that if you have nothing, you at least have your own hair. Then she would put her finger in her hair and enact the motion of pulling some out. That would be enough to show payment to the Creator.

Casey says that he and Lillian still talk to Mary; they still ask "What would Mom do?" And they continue to visit her grave. Years ago, Casey promised Mary that, with her passing, he would love and look after Lillian, and he has done so, absolutely.

South of the rodeo grounds is an old stony homestead site with various signs of the original occupancy, including some gnarled but still fruiting orchard trees and an Acme cookstove next to a wire fence, just off the road. On the open oven door, or up on the enamelled warming shelf, a large yellow-bellied marmot could sometimes be seen, lying there comfortably, taking in the view and the sunshine as if he owned the place and had done so for marmot eons. If you stopped and stared too long, he disappeared into the bowels of the stove until you moved on. There were other marmots in less monumental marmot homes nearby—the site of at least one was actually under the roadway, but only a short distance from patches of blooming spring sage buttercups.

When buttercups bloom, sandhill cranes fly north in great wavering, slow-moving vees high up at the top of the sky. On a quiet evening, you can hear them. They are barely visible and hard to see, but you can spot them if you look.

ASKING ROCK

In our day we learned by listening to the land.
The land talks if you know how to listen.
—Louis Phillips, Lytton, BC, 1993

I AM BECOMING INCREASINGLY CONNECTED TO A SMALL RIVER SYSTEM IN southwest British Columbia called the Stein Valley. All but one of my frequent visits there have been short—usually a day to walk in to some of the rock-writing sites up-valley and out again, or even less if I'm just after a taste of the place. So I have only really focused on the lower stretches of the river and canyon and a certain lively entity down along that way called Asking Rock. My appreciation and understanding of the area have been a long time evolving, well over thirty years in fact. In that time I've come to feel and know some of the ecological and cultural richness of the place and, little by little, some of its subtle spiritual impact also. But having only dipped into a few corners of it here and there, I would not say I know the valley well. It would take a lifetime of walking throughout, in all seasons, to know the place in depth.

The Stein River and most of its main tributaries flow southwest and west to east, generally, to empty into the Fraser River a short distance north of the town of Lytton. The river's headwaters rise on some of the high east-facing slopes of the Coast Range, east of Lillooet Lake, and are very much under the influence of the rain-bearing West Coast climate, as are the core upper and central reaches of the main Stein drainage. Forests there are untouched old growth, with dominant tree species ranging from western hemlock and Engelmann spruce to Interior Douglas fir, and tall cottonwoods along the flood plains. Farther east, as the valley drops, the rains diminish and the warm Interior summer climate increasingly prevails; the main tree species there are dry-belt Douglas fir and ponderosa pine. Small groves of red cedar are evident in shady, moisture-holding bends in the river and stream systems, as are poplar groves and lodgepole pine on the sidehills. Alpine fir and whitebark pine grow at the sub-alpine timber edges on the high mountain slopes. The series of ecosystems or "biogeoclimatic zones," in transition from glaciers and alpine rock to dry-land big sagebrush, is unusually diverse, with as many as twelve distinct sub-zones, ecologists state. The overall length of the Stein drainage system, from mountain divides to the mouth of the river, is only about thirty-six miles.

The lower Stein area, including the narrow, vulnerable, lower canyon, is mercifully unlogged and unintruded by roads, and the impact of mining exploration and development has been slight. Road building through that confined area would have been severely destructive. But a ten-thousand-year-old trail, in use since the retreat of the glaciers, runs east–west, connecting Nlaka'pamux (Thompson) and St'at'imc (Lillooet) territories. That path bypassed the steep rock walls and precarious trails of the Fraser Canyon and served as an alternative route from the Interior to the lower Fraser Valley. The old trail is redolent with history and human usage; the signs are subtle but frequent if you watch for them. We feel the impact of those centuries of feet, coming and going, as we walk it. And late in the day, when the shadows go long and we grow tired and more a part of the trail's flow, we might sense the trees and tall shrubs, especially species that grow densely—fir, cottonwoods, willows, red-osier dogwood, lodgepole pine—leaning in behind us as we pass through.

The Stein Valley in its entirety is an ecological jewel and not to be taken for granted. It is the last intact watershed of any significant size in the southwest Interior, and its present status as a protected provincial park was hard-won over too many years, a fact we may now tend to forget. The attempts to open

Reaction ferry crossing the Fraser River near Lytton. Photo courtesy of Marne St. Claire.

the Stein for logging in the 1980s triggered strong, sustained resistance, and when it was determined that the extraction of timber from the valley was not economical and would necessitate government (i.e., taxpayer paid) subsidies to the logging companies, the struggle to protect this glorious place was won. The park's current title, Stein Valley Nlaka'pamux Heritage Provincial Park, reflects that victory and the involvement of a wide range of activists from local First Nations bands to environmental groups and committed individuals. The park is designated a First Nations land reserve and heritage site and is co-managed by the BC Parks branch and the Lytton Indian Band.

Don Brooks and I walked through a portion of that Stein country back in 1980. That walk, one of our more strenuous, was our fifth summertime backpacking trip together and initiated a series of annual explorations of various parts of the vast Chilcotin region west of the Fraser River and north of Lillooet. We have done a week-long walking trip together up in that wild country virtually every August since.

This particular venture involved two cars: one to park and leave at the east end of the Stein River trail; the other to drive within walking distance of our first camp at Blowdown Pass up off the Duffy Lake Road some distance southwest of Lillooet. We crossed over to the west side of the Fraser River on the little reaction ferry upriver from Lytton, then drove north past Earlscourt Farm for two or three miles and turned west onto a short side road to drop off my car—we'd pick it up a week later at the conclusion of our walk. The track in is marked at the start by a couple of kekuli holes on the bench above the riverbed, water-rounded river cobbles half-buried in the roadbed in front of us, and clumps of shiny-leafed snowbrush (*Ceanothus*) on either side. When we parked and shut the motor off, the sound of the Stein River was an immediate presence, a force, even at low water, rushing and roaring its way out of the mouth of the canyon. We could spot the famous trail curving west through riparian willow and osier dogwood brush, and there was faint bird song, partially lost in the river noise. This was our first contact with the Stein Valley, and we could see immediately that it was a strong and lively place, well worn by wild nature and by humans, but still very much in balance with itself; the human touch had been light so far.

We carried on north in Don's creaky Volkswagen Bug up the slow, windy, west-side road to Seton Creek and the town of Lillooet. I find this drive fascinating for the beauty of the Fraser River Canyon, the fir slopes and open pine flats on both sides, and all the signs of long human use. The benches upriver are dotted with old homesteads, most of them Indian and going back over a century, some still inhabited and used, others long abandoned. Much of the country from below the Stein River to Lillooet and points north is Indian Reserve land. In pre-contact times, Lytton, known to the Nlaka'pamux as Kumsheen or Lkamtci'n, and situated at the point where the great Fraser and Thompson Rivers meet, was seen as the centre of the Nlaka'pamux world, a place where energies, human and wild nature, were concentrated, a place where old myth-stories abide. Driving through, and seeing and sensing the area, it is not difficult to feel why.

At Seton Creek in St'at'imc land, within sight of the great rock-writing panels above the railroad tracks and the sloped mountain goat pastures high above that, we turned west up the Duffy Lake Road. A half hour later we turned off onto a narrow mining and logging road above Blowdown Creek, the route to Blowdown Pass. The sky was dark and heavy with impending precipitation.

By the time we got our tent up and dry firewood gathered (a fixation of mine), snow was falling: big fat snowflakes, a sky full of them. If I remember right (and it's been thirty-three years now), Don and I stood in the lee of a clutch of alpine fir trees not much taller than ourselves, drinking a little brandy I carried for just such emergencies and enjoying the snowy silence of the place. Later, as the clouds cleared, we admired the sight of the snow-white ridgeline above us, curving knife-edged against a fresh blue sky, our enthusiasm perhaps intensified by our hopes for a dry tomorrow. In the dark late that night, both of us, fully awake, stock-still, barely breathing, listened as some heavy-footed, bearish animal, definitely not a deer, passed through the brush close by the tent. At new light the snow had mostly disappeared, leaving us no clear tracks to find and identify.

That day a thin fog prevailed, with light but persistent rain falling, and we walked through it to the top of bald Gott Peak. The morning after that, having cooked and consumed the weightiest food items in our packs (Don and I refer to that exercise as "eating down"), we set off along a mining track that accompanied Cottonwood Creek on its lively way to the Stein River thirteen-plus miles east by southeast of us. Our plan was to follow the track for about five miles, then walk up a side branch south past the site of the disused Silver Queen Mine partway up. We would camp somewhere in that vicinity, then climb and walk the ridge above the next day, before dropping down the steep south-facing sidehill to the Stein.

We soon passed some particularly rich sub-alpine flower gardens, thick with alpine flowers—tall white eriogonums, anemones, Indian paintbrush, lupines, late arnicas, purple asters, blue monkshood—and some of the fattest hoary marmots we've ever seen. The short summer was at full climax. Most marmots nearby were up on their hind legs doing their job, whistling the news of our presence across the hillside; they were only mildly alarmed but determined to alert the entire colony, just in case, ducking out of sight as we walked by. Our route took us below the actual heart of marmot land, a lush, south-facing, hanging valley known as Marmot Gardens.

The waters of two great rivers, the muddy Fraser and the clear Thompson, merge at Lytton. Photo courtesy of Marne St. Claire.

In the afternoon, after a right turn and slow trudge up the Silver Queen road, we came to a little flat by a small pond at a sharp bend in the track. The open pond edges closest to us were covered with a small, verdant, low-growing species of plant, and at centre stage, only a few dozen feet away from us and dominating the view, a small, light-toned grizzly bear was busy grazing. She (or he?) had obviously heard us coming and seemed now to be intent on digging into those mats of little plants, a surprisingly delicate operation considering the length of those great claws of hers. We stood there quietly, trying to get a good read on the animal and thinking through our options. She'd look over at us for a moment or two, raise her nose and sniff the air a little, clearly not alarmed, then resume her excavating and munching on plant roots or corms or whatever she was after. I strongly suspect they were late-growing spring beauties (Indian potatoes); we were at their

Grizzly bears. Photo courtesy of Larry Travis, Raincoast Images, and Jane Woodland and Chris Genovali, Raincoast Conservation Foundation.

typical elevation, and I understand their bulb-like, marble-sized, sweet corms are high on bears' preferred list. Making a meal on Indian spuds has to be labour-intensive, even for a small bear. Of course, I had no chance to get down on my knees and check the crop out for myself.

Don and I came to a silent decision, mainly by slow hand signals. We had two choices: back up and crash through thick brush and windfalls off-road to bypass the creature entirely, or slowly walk up the open road past her at an increasing angle away from where she was feeding. We chose the latter—it seemed so much easier. And our ursine acquaintance appeared to not mind us at all. We talked to her quietly, avoiding anything more than minimal eye contact, and walked slowly by—no quick moves for us—all the while indicating by our body motion and sideways direction that we were no threat to her whatsoever. She glanced at us a couple of times, barely pausing from her extended meal; it seemed evident she knew we meant her no harm. After we gained a little distance, Don and I picked up our usual walking rate and carried on up the hillside.

The slope there is steep; there were virtually no suitably flat places to camp, so we chose the next best thing at a rocky turnout on the track only a few hundred yards above our new neighbour and settled down for the night. We, usually Don, cooked by open fire in those days, and that we did again as evening set in; we ate our fine dinner seated on a log with our backs to the fire, keeping an eye on our hard-working associate. She'd raise her head from foraging and look up at us occasionally, and at dusk she turned and ambled slowly off into dark timber at the far end of the pond.

Our campsite overlooked a small but steep gully below us. That evening I shinnied up a tall hemlock sapling above the gully, our hank of light rope in my teeth. I tied my end of it to the tree's trunk with a good bowline knot, then, together, Don and I heave-hoed our food bag sky-high. We were taking no chances. The next morning early, as we got the fire and coffee going, our grizzly comrade emerged from the dark trees to pick up where she had left off the evening before. We packed and began our grind up and along the ridge farther east; our backs were mostly turned, but as far as we could tell she never looked up.

By lunch it was raining, and we hunkered down under a tree to rest and eat. Partway through, I glanced up to see a decades-old martin trap, sprung and hanging by its chain from a branch just above our heads. That trapper, whoever he was, had to be a very tough man to climb that steep slope in snowshoes and deep snow in the cold of winter. Later, as we began to descend, near the cliffy southeast end of the ridge we had been following, I almost stepped on a mountain goat relaxing in the lee of a semi-rotten windfall log below me. He took off like a shot to his escape cliff close by. We peered around the rock face to see if we could spot him, and there the goat was on the far side of the rock, peering right back at us to determine what kind of a threat we might actually be. He seemed to be a lone goat, leading us to think it was an old male.

We were navigating by compass, map, sight and common sense. But dense rain clouds had socked in the narrow lake—Kent Lake by name—on the south side of the valley high above the Stein, which we intended to use as a directional guide as we picked our way down off the ridge. Bushwhacking down steep slopes with full packs through dense azalea and huckleberry thickets is hard work, especially on the knees, and we had to retrace our route once or twice to avoid topping out at the high end of some precipice. We had over 4000 feet of elevation to lose and were pretty much spent by the time we reached the valley bottom. As semi-predicted, we found ourselves only a short distance up the Stein River from the mouth of Cottonwood Creek and the campsite we had planned to reach.

Late and mind-numb, we started in to set up camp. It was there, in those moments, that Don and I had the only sharp words we have had on well over thirty trips together, before and since, and actually it was I, and I only, who uttered them. I looked up from emptying the tent bag to see the mighty Don B (and he is a big man) coming down full force with my good camp axe onto a piece of soon-to-be firewood; the problem was that the metal-studded, leather, axe-head cover was still attached, and I work hard to keep my axe-edge sharp. I won't repeat my expletive, but it was short, harsh and, some would say, rude, but Don took it well, fortunately. He was probably too beat to react with any fervour.

The trail from Cottonwood Creek east along the north side of the valley to the cable crossing is ten miles long; much of it borders on flood plains along a mainly slow-moving stretch of the river. Behind us, not far west of the confluence of Cottonwood with the Stein, was Scudamore Creek, the south branch of which is also known as Battle Creek. Somewhere along its length, closer to its mouth, I assume, was the site of a famous battle that took place about 1850, part of ongoing conflicts between Nlaka'pamux from around Lytton and St'at'imc warriors from the Mount Currie section of the Lillooet Valley, over the mountains to the west.

This part of the route is historically resonant in other ways. When we first walked through here in 1980, we had no knowledge of several red-ochre rock-writing sites along this section of the trail, including a cave site somewhere up the hillside. There are even some sparse pictographic images, found fairly recently, on an old blaze in the living wood of a cedar tree near the crossing downriver. We were using John Corner's pictographs guide then, a fine handbook that I had referenced religiously for years on sites across various parts of southern BC. In the 1990s, Richard Daly and Chris Arnett (with Annie York) wrote *They Write Their Dreams on the Rock Forever* (1993), a wonderfully rich book on all the known Stein River rock writings. Their treatise has much general information and cultural background, as well as abundant detail on well-known and newly noted sites. The

> *We were navigating by compass, map, sight and common sense.*

book is especially graced by Annie York's detailed stories and translations of the groups of painted images and symbols depicted on the pictograph panels; there are eighteen known sites—some extensive, some small and hidden—up and down the river. Ms. York, who died in 1993, was thoroughly educated and interested in the old ways and could read the range of Stein rock writings, copied and presented to her by Daly and Arnett, as if she was reading a newspaper. I have written in greater detail about Annie York in a chapter of my first book, *Stranger Wycott's Place*.

On the fifth evening of that 1980 trip, Don and I camped just short of the cable crossing; the following morning we passed over to the south side of the Stein River. The cable car set-up in those days was decrepit, and there were several stories about mishaps; we soon had our own short tale to add. The two hitches to a trouble-free river crossing for us were that the cable-car seat was falling apart and that Don, as he was pulling himself across, dropped the pull-rope. This meant I had to do most of the hard work of pulling large Don and his large pack, inch by back-bending, teeth-gritting inch, up a slack cable on the considerably uphill second half of the enterprise. It reminded me, too much, of pulling steel-rope strawline on sweaty sidehill logging shows. Don owes me big.

We passed Klein's cabin and, a short time later, Earl's cabin at Earl Creek. There are more pictograph rocks somewhere close to the latter place, but I did not know that then. The trail is excellent. Another two or three miles of steady, pleasant walking brought us to an old stopping and camping place where the path passes between several granite boulders not far from the river. On one of the boulders, head-high and marred by spalling from fires set too close, is a group of painted rock writings with different animal, bird and human-like figures and various other symbols. Annie York interprets these writings in much rich detail and states emphatically that this set depicts a dream about a boy who travelled to the moon. Two of the men pictured carry bows, and a deer is obviously pierced by an arrow. Those stick people we see are actually Spider People, and they are in the process of showing humans the advantages of deer hunting with this new technology. Our ancient hunter-gatherer ancestors, it seems, were taught woods knowledge and techniques by supernatural beings, often presented to us as animals or animal-people, back then in dream time, so the old myth-tales tell us.

That spalled boulder site is a short distance from the greatest of all the rock-writing sites on the Stein River, and Don and I were looking forward to viewing them, courtesy of John Corner. The site is named Ts'ets'ekw, meaning "writings" or "a picture or mark of any kind." Ts'ets'ekw is an impressive complex of mostly low, dark, vertical stone panels filled with many dozens of red-ochre images along a cliff bottom near the river. The short path to them off the main trail is easily missed. Pictographic sites seem usually to be set in places that are either quite visible—often along major, sun-facing trails, for example—or in places felt to be of power, like caves and canyons. Such gaps or cracks in the surface of the earth were recognized by the ancestors in old myth times as apertures to the spirit underworld, shaman's tunnels to places of power and potential wealth. Old-time myth heroes ventured down such tunnels at risk of death and dismemberment to gain strength and knowledge for themselves and the betterment of their people. The narrow rocky canyon on the lower Stein, an obvious, audible and moving force of its own, seems to be one such entrance place.

Ts'ets'ekw is about aboriginal vision questing, also known as spirit questing, so the Daly/Arnett/York texts inform us. Seekers, in their search for strength and protection in an uncertain and frequently dangerous world, performed various rites and deprivations alone near locations of concentrated spiritual power, like Ts'ets'ekw. In these wild, isolated and holy places, such searchers, often young Nlaka'pamux men on their way to manhood, went without food, water, warmth, sleep and human company over several (usually four but perhaps many) days and nights in order to be sufficiently mind-altered and

Rock writing at Ts'ets'ekw up the Stein River. Photo courtesy of Marne St. Claire.

open to spirit forces. It was essential for their training that they not be interrupted. They would pray, meditate, sweat, chant and sing through much of the duration to attract guardian spirits and animal powers, and insightful dreams and visions that might bring strength, guidance and protection for themselves and their relatives. Some of these seekers would be warriors about to set off up the Stein trail for another round of armed struggle with St'at'imc people from the Lillooet River Valley to the west, hoping and working for courage and victories in the forays ahead. Some could be hunters looking to avoid hunger and starvation. Others might be would-be healers, medicine doctors seeking healing lore, or shamans after esoteric powers to increase their spiritual authority.

Vision questing alone in the bush was far more than the enactment of a rite of passage, more profound than a relatively predictable cultural event. Such ventures were intense, challenging, sometimes terror-inducing and potentially dangerous for all participants. To overcome their fears and any adversaries that might present themselves as they sought visions and spiritual help, seekers needed to summon all their courage and perseverance, and any possible support, subtle or material, along the way. The proceedings demanded a high degree of surrender to forces in wild nature much greater than the participants. The old shamanistic ways, back then and even now, present a world of possibilities to us; to learn to transcend our fears and the sense of powerlessness that can come from fear is soul shaking, mind shaping, and ultimately transformative.

Rock writings and paintings depict individual vision searches in symbolic detail and underscore the link between living individuals and the supernatural. They are a kind of re-creation and demonstration that visions and spirit visitations occur; painted images become the quest-creatures experienced, in the same way that masked dancers become the animals they are dancing. Humans, animals and other wild beings merge. Fundamentally, there is no disconnection between consciousnesses. The red paint used is made from powdered red ochre and pitch, mixed with saliva into a paste; the colour red is evocative of the power of all life. The range of images and symbols is wide, and there is a degree of standardization about most of them that allows us to view them now as a kind of writing, sufficiently interpretable that Annie York, for example, could read them so impressively. One recurring image at Ts'ets'ekw is a certain two-headed, winged creature, looking vaguely like an owl, with a deer or mountain sheep under each curved wing as if they had been captured or killed. This mysterious creature is likely a mythic equivalent of a rubber boa snake, sometimes called "the two-headed snake," found in warmer, dryer parts of the Interior. It is, apparently, a hunting symbol of considerable significance. The visual power of this image is self-evident.

Don and I came away deeply impressed by the writing panels at the main Ts'ets'ekw site; I'm sure we would have appreciated the rock writings at the lower site, several hundred yards downriver, as well, but neither we nor John Corner knew they existed then. Part of the reason for that could be that the trail east from Ts'ets'ekw traverses a steep hillside high above the river, and the side route down off the trail to the site at water's edge is obscure and somewhat awkward to use. Once there, the diligent searcher will find several small groups of images on near-vertical rock faces scattered along the river for two or three hundred feet. Some of them are located high up, out of reach, and created with considerable difficulty, no doubt; as well, some figures are faint and need the right light to be spotted and observed. If it is late spring and the river is high, viewers may find themselves prevented from seeing them at all. A recurring theme in this set of rock-writing panels is bear, represented by paw prints, nine or ten of them, grizzlies mainly, painted in the standardized manner. Until fairly recently, grizzly sightings were common down the lower Stein.

By the most eastern of the main writing panels, the river bends, its conformation caused in part by a long talus slope of large angular rocks, a great slide known as the Devil's Staircase. The path up and across it is rough, but from its higher points there is a dramatic view of the canyon and river up the valley. The slope is steep and in constant slow motion downward, rock by rock, into the river as the fast-moving waters erode the slide's underpinnings. Often there are new fallen rocks that need to be rolled or pushed off the trail so that the route remains open and usable.

Down by the river, below the switchbacks on the east side of the slide, is an attractive campsite. Not far east of there on one of our walks up from Asking Rock, my partner Marne and I met three people, First Nations folks, from the Lillooet Valley (Mount Currie, I believe). They were two elders, man and wife, and their not-so-young son, gentle people, walking in to that camping place to fast and pray and, they hoped, receive spiritual strength and inspiration. The younger man needed big help to rid himself of the relentless weight of addiction, and his mother and father were travelling up there with him in support. We had a warm exchange with them, standing there on the trail in the trees, the steady river-sound behind us. We concluded our short time together by giving our most heartfelt wishes to them for good health and success in their quest. May they be well and thrive! May all seekers on this land be well and thrive.

From the great slide, it is a walk of less than three miles down the Stein to the cluster of worn rock surfaces and cliff faces called Asking Rock. When Don and I came to the end of our long walk across country from Blowdown Pass in 1980, we set up our final camp a couple of hundred yards upriver from that place. We are usually tidy campers, but the signs of our cobblestone fire ring, as modest as it was, were visible on a little twin-flower-covered flat between the trail and the river for years. Twin-flower is one of the world's tiniest shrubs and, as the shamanistic way of seeing once was, is ubiquitous around the northern hemisphere.

Asking Rock is another of those places of power along the river, and the best known of all the Stein pictograph sites. As we approach, the rock "looms

Asking Rock by the lower Stein River. Photo courtesy of Marne St. Claire.

up like a sentinel," as Chris Arnett aptly describes it. The trail runs close beneath, and passing by it we cannot help but see that the soft sedimentary rock has been worn into basins, hollows, ledges and small shallow caves by the river as it eroded its way over centuries to its present level. There are weathered rock paintings on several concave vertical walls, most of them too worn to easily discern and interpret. Vision quests occurred near this place, and young people, boys and girls both, came to undergo puberty rituals, so the old rock writings indicate and elders tell us. Passersby may notice cracks and little holes and pockets in the lichen-covered rock and, tucked into some of them, small offerings of tobacco, sagebrush leaves and coins. Clearly, this is a place where people have come to pray, probably for thousands of years.

In *Larry Emile's Drum*, a story in my second book, *Old Lives*, Secwepemc elder Percy Rosette proclaims, "There are some places around this country where we pray." Certain lively places, like Asking Rock, become acknowledged and sanctified for their power and the glory of their settings, and as time passes, by long practice as people trek in to such locations seeking connection, help and guidance.

Birth Rock, the Stein River and the ten-thousand-year-old trail west to Lillooet country. Photo courtesy of Marne St. Claire.

Many of those spiritually minded visitors are of the belief that when we come to such a place to sojourn and pray, we are bound to leave something, however small, in return for the privilege of seeking assistance, giving thanks or even just being there. Hunters in earlier times, and perhaps in the present, made offerings in these places to ensure good weather, safety and fruitful hunting. The nature of the interactions of spirit in wild nature is one of balance and exchange. If we have come to pray, we must offer up something of ourselves symbolic of our willingness to expose our inner, subtle being, our soul, to the powers and beneficence and rigours of great nature.

As a backdrop, the roar of the Stein River is a constant, its sound reflecting against the rocks and rock walls that comprise Asking Rock. One of those ancillary rocks, a large granite boulder between the writings and the river, is known as Birth Rock. In earlier times, pregnant women came here to take shelter in the narrow space underneath it, to give birth to their babies and, afterwards, to bathe them in the little rock pools by the edge of the river.

There are other rock-writing sites in the vicinity of the lower Stein River: a single small painting in a little stone alcove across the river, visible from Asking Rock; a massive pecked boulder at high-water mark on the west bank of the Fraser River not far from the Stein; and another set of well-defined rock paintings on an outcrop near a net-setting and dip-netting site within view of the village of Lytton downriver. I myself found a very small and obscure painting on a dark rock in bush close to the bridge over the Stein; I'm sure its location is known to local people.

The whole area is rich with history, myth, holy power places, and signs of long human habitation. There are numerous kekuli pithouse holes on both sides of the Stein mouth and elsewhere up and down the Fraser, and there are or were several old, usually small, church buildings still standing here and there along the big river as well. Don Brooks and I noted the rickety old St. David's Anglican church at Stryen Reserve when we drove north in 1980; it was on a definite lean then, and was later torn down for reasons of safety. And between the east and west forks of upper Stryen Creek, a tributary of the Stein that merges close to Asking Rock, K'ek'/azik', otherwise known as Mount Roach, stands tall at 8670 feet. Louis Phillips described the mountain as "our school." K'ek'/azik' is believed to have supernatural qualities, and in earlier times young people went there for inspiration and spirit power. The backcountry around K'ek'/azik' was known to harbour land and water mysteries, tricky spirit-beings capable of shape-shifting and deception, and potentially dangerous; to see these apparitions was considered an evil omen and a risk of sickness and death for the viewer. Visitors out in that country were careful to deport themselves with caution and careful manners.

In those primal, pre-contact, shamanistic times, all elements of great nature were perceived to be alive, lively, interconnected and responsive. Over the now many decades of my life, I have come to experience this way of seeing and know it to be accessible and real; such awareness requires only that we relax, drop our old habit-judgments and stay open to possibilities. Spending extended time alone in wild backcountry places underlines our vulnerability and refines our attention. We learn to see and feel that the old sites—K'ek'/azik', Asking Rock, Ts'ets'ekw and all the rest—are living parts of a much larger, lively, complex, wild whole; the Stein River and its many branches flow through it all and sustain it. We can see that rock writings and their natural settings up and down the Stein, and elsewhere, are indivisible, their power and significance an ecological fact.

Should we choose to view and treat comparable sites across the land as separate from their settings and their surrounding watersheds—and we do so constantly—we render them inert, static, devoid of meaning. Thus we become more likely to use these places in an uncaring and exploitive manner, the same deadly way we have treated so much of the rest of the wild world for so long. If we had merely protected some of the rock writings in the lower Stein canyon as artifacts, a real possibility back in the 1980s, each painting and panel would have become the equivalent of preserved dead wild animals displayed, essence-less, behind glass in museums. The writings would have become merely red-ochre marks on a rock wall.

So for the Stein River and all its tributaries to have acquired provincial park status and some degree of protection is a conservationist miracle that must merit our ongoing gratitude and vigilance. Though change is perpetual, the Stein watershed is a wild system in balance with itself; as such, it is perfect, and a great gift to us and to all life. We can only be thankful for that.

I have found writing about rock writing and vision or spirit questing to be difficult at times. For starters, the only real way to understand a vision quest is to have fully experienced the process personally. Obviously I have not, so any sharpness of mind on the topic comes slowly. I have had to learn more thoroughly to be quiet and to meditate for maximum clarity each time I sit down to write about pictograph and petroglyph sites and what they may present and represent. It seems as if the essential energies of these places demand more deference than I am used to expressing before I am able to usefully continue my work. To the extent that I am un-self-focused, free and patiently surrendered to the process, acceptably meaningful writing occurs, however doggedly. Why shouldn't efforts to explore the austere and subtle practice of seeking visions and guidance alone in wild places be difficult?

Vision or spirit questing was and is an expression of an ancient way of seeing and being that is set in here-and-now myth time, dream time, where, as Robert Bringhurst states, "all existents are alive." That viewpoint is shamanistic, a way to see the world that we linear-minded, time-bound folks of European descent, among many others, knew and practised for tens of thousands of years, but have since forgotten with the advent of advanced agriculture, the great religions and science. Now we deny and denigrate myth and myth time. In coming to an understanding of vision seeking, we might easily incorporate some sense of the demands and struggles, the connectedness and even, perhaps, the awe and wonder experienced by the seeker.

Since my first visit to the lower Stein River with Don, I've walked the three-mile trail from river mouth to upriver rock-writing sites a number of times, either alone, with hiking friends or with my partner Marne, and I remain entranced by the place. Every trip is interesting. No two trips there are the same, the Stein canyon country in its diversity and rocky ruggedness is unfailingly attractive, and I will continue to come here from time to time for as long as I am mobile. The walks in to Asking Rock and up the valley to the main pictograph sites have become small pilgrimages. I treat them accordingly. I come especially in the bright months of April and May, when the woods are alive with moving birds and the signs of spring unfolding, and more northern, high-elevated regions of the province are still seized with winter.

Sometimes I come, alone or with Marne, just to stop for an hour or two at Asking Rock to say thank you, and always to get a taste of the lower valley in one of its seasonal variations. We acknowledge the old sites and the heroes who helped preserve this beautiful valley: James Teit, who so respectfully and thoroughly recorded the old cultures over a century ago; Annie York, the great student and interpreter of old Indian ways; all the Nlaka'pamux elders, past and present, who have known this place so deeply over so many years; the various modern-day anthropologists, Richard Daly, Chris Arnett, Wendy Wickwire et al., for their professional dedication; and the many activists and supporters who fought for park status and protection, and without whom the liveliness of the Stein River drainage, the canyon, benches, flats and mountains, would have been radically diminished by the effects of even a short-lived logging intrusion.

Five local Nlaka'pamux elders who loved the Stein Valley and worked toward its conservation, and who have passed on, have had their lives acknowledged in a special manner. They are commemorated in an open stand of fir and old ponderosa pine just off the Stein trail a half mile east of the great slide. Four small wooden plaques, artfully crafted, are attached to the trunk of one especially venerable yellow pine at the centre of the grove. Their dedications are personal and unique to each character. The respect that each of these elders has earned is experienced fully in the quiet of such a still and timeless setting.

Plaques commemorating Nlaka'pamux elders for their dedication to the Stein Valley. Photo courtesy of John Schreiber.

Currently, park managers and elders around Lytton are asking us to demonstrate our respect by choosing to not leave litter at Asking Rock, as some passing hikers have done, leaving their sticks, trail-worn shoes, candles, candy wrappers, cigarettes and other detritus at the base of the rock, beneath the old spirit paintings. We have a responsibility to be mindful here, though personally I see no harm in a pinch of tobacco scattered to the winds when we offer up our acknowledgments and gratitude. "You must leave something," the old folks would say.

As so much of what's left of wild nature across the earth is disappearing or threatened, it demands our vigilance and right action or we'll lose it. We'll lose what we never owned, what we never could own. We'll lose it without even knowing we lost it. Without wild nature, wild species, wild places and wilderness itself, natural diversity, not to mention our future survival and the integrity of our souls, is at risk. Are we aware of the annual wild bird survey trends in North America these years? Do we know that the population numbers of so many species—shore and grassland birds, aerial insectivores, swallows, flycatchers, warblers, nighthawks, even meadowlarks—are dropping steadily? Do we understand what those shrinking numbers mean? Does it matter? Do we care?

This coming spring, Marne and I will stop by Asking Rock to give thanks for the gift of a healthy Svea, new baby daughter of son Michael and Jenny, come brightly to join our world. When we were passing through the area last fall, Marne walked in to stand by the rock and pray for a safe birth for mother and child. Now she will be expressing her considerable relief and gratitude. We will probably walk upriver to Ts'ets'ekw while we are there. Marne says, "I love the earth with the layers of pine needles under my feet; they give a spring to the walk."

Perhaps the most lasting image for me, among many such here in the lower Stein, is of Marne returning from a walk up the valley one early April afternoon some years back. The day was late; the shadows were reaching. She was walking back down through the open woods some distance behind me in that lighthearted way of hers, not hurrying, but striding along, face angled to the light sky, her head turning slowly side to side, scanning and absorbing the beauty: those ponderosa benches and bouldered terraces we walk through; the long ridgelines above, silhouetted; the high peaks in the back, white with sunlit snow and ice; clean, spring air fresh on our faces; river-sound in our ears. Such sensibilities, such connections inspire us all. This Stein River land abides with the fullness of its residing spirit life: trees, rocks, swamps, creeks, mountains, the river, the rock writings, the twin-flowers on that little flat at Asking Rock. Living energies all, each entity with its own wild nature, inclination and expression. Personified, they are gods.

Two ways, two ways to see.

ALONE AT LONE CREEK

That the self advances and confirms the
myriad things is called delusion.
That the myriad things advance and confirm
the self is enlightenment.
                    —Master Dogen, 13th century

SOMEWHERE IN THE INTERIOR OF THIS "GREAT LONE LAND," AS WILLIAM Francis Butler described and named the wide open Canadian West back in 1873, there is a place I choose to call Lone Creek. This site has its own intrinsic beauty and vulnerability, which has been subtly cultured by human use and by time so that its essence is of the finest. The seasons have weathered it. The essential liveliness of the place is still intact, but Lone Creek will be more secure, I think, if I do not refer to it by its true name.

A number of places, like Lone Creek, are best not named or, if they are, revealed with careful discretion. Just as some personal details are private, so the sanctity of a place may need to be protected. Some places—small alpine valleys, certain creek systems, pond edges and most wetlands, for example—can have an essence so clean, so assailable, that the imperative to respect and protect is plain. Coarse attention and casual actions are likely to lead to destruction: the more we tread on a sub-alpine meadow in spring runoff, the more it is defiled and reduced; when we run our ATV through a swamp just once, that swamp is altered, some sections wrecked. What is required is full attention to our actions as much as we are able. Such mindfulness is respectful and may indicate the need to practise least use, "Ahimsa," least harm.

Lone Creek has become a meditation for me. If a place like Lone Creek is not inert, not mere backdrop, then it, in all its detailed aspects, must have some form of living expression; perhaps we are becoming a part of its expression. There may be some kind of reciprocity here. Part of the connection may be that there is an opportunity to hear a place speak. It may be an active participant in this story: the details are lively. It could well be that when we stop the chatter, inner and outer, and let a place express its own being, we can reflect its truth most clearly, and consequently hear our own truth more thoroughly.

In this "Great Lone Land" there are many such places that can bite into the heart with poignancy, that stop us in our own footsteps. Many of us know such places. Perhaps this land is so huge and powerful, and so much of it is so implacably wild, that we feel small in comparison. Perhaps the vestiges of past human efforts crumbling into the soil evoke a response in us. We are reminded of our fragility, our aloneness. Such awareness is sobering; such humbling puts us "in our place" and keeps us from hubris, self worship, complacency and the consequent incapacity to look and see and understand. When we are modest we listen more carefully and hear.

Perhaps the vestiges of past human efforts crumbling into the soil evoke a response in us.

What I hear and see at Lone Creek is about seclusion and fineness: most everything is refined at Lone Creek. In the wake of the ice age, after the major melting, the first settlers were plants, then birds and animals, and eventually the first peoples, and they have all in their various ways settled in. There is a balance here that two more centuries of seasons and weathering and modern, post-contact human involvement have maintained so far. The serious disturbances of the last hundred and fifty years have been limited.

Warren Menhinick and I were talking over at Gold Bridge some time back. We were commenting on a few of these places that people don't know much, or ignore, and which might lose something for being noticed and used. We agreed there were a variety of such unknown places across this land, some wild, some not so, some of them passed through but not seen, others unusual or even strange, some long abandoned by humans, nearly all of them attractive. Warren told me of one that moved him: "You should go to Lone Creek," he said. "You'd like it. There are wild horses down there and an old church nobody's used in a hundred years. It's a helluva road going in. Don't be sitting on the passenger side if you don't like heights." Warren had been a guide-outfitter for much of his adult life and always had lots of horses to feed and maintain. He has a hard-working, upbeat wife, Casie; a bunch of lively young kids; a wide range of skills, including deep horse knowing; and a quiet sense of humour.

So I went to Lone Creek. I got in my Pathfinder and drove. It was May and fresh. Life was beginning again; the birds were moving north and the weather was not yet too hot.

THE ROAD IN, WINDING DOWN OFF THE HIGH, LOGGING TRUNK ROAD OUT OF standing timber into open parkland, is not too bad at first. Then, as big sage and rabbitbush start to show, the track gets awesome, in the truest sense of that overworked word. The hillside is sheer in places, and the road turns suddenly skinny. It meanders and twists around a rocky point at a narrowing of the river canyon I am paralleling. My dear partner, Marne, is a brave passenger, but if she'd been riding shotgun with me, she'd have been on the far side, looking out and down over 1700 mainly vertical feet of empty, mind-bending space in places, with no turnouts or wide places and barely a firm, reassuring shoulder in sight, unless she leaned right out to look—a move that has absolutely no chance of happening, whatsoever. There are just a few friendly dry-belt fir or ponderosa pine to give solidity, solace and some perspective, but the view is limited to the far side of the canyon, and to the river, looking small, a long way down. I am glad, for the moment, that Marne is not with me. Later, when I describe the place, I tell her, "Marne, unless you walk that long walk in, I do not believe you will be seeing Lone Creek."

Other than its narrowness in places, the road surface is all right: hard, not too rough or steep, but for a few short stretches of angled slough-off on the uphill (that is to say, up-cliff) side, and obviously not frequently used. However, I would not want to test its clay and gravel surface after a few days' rain. "Unforgiving" is one word that comes to mind; "chute" is another. My main concern is meeting somebody. I would be extremely loath to try backing up, especially in the dark of night when the shoulders are not visible. A wrong choice, several long and mighty bounces, and you'd be in the river for all time, the quick route, in fragments, to the great sea. Fortunately, there is no tire sign of any kind, fresh or old, just deer and horse spoor. The horse tracks I check are shoeless. I expect that deer, still wintering in scattered herds on the low benches, use this route as a regular convenience.

I pick my way in, and after a quarter mile of goat track and a whitening of my knuckles, the road opens out onto a boulder-strewn bench, burnt dry by heat of summers and the oven-like aspects of this great gorge, one face of which I have just passed across. This rough bench is one of a series stretching north into haze for miles, a succession of blue-grey sagebrush slopes, all with that same glacial-lake-bottom tilt, that same slightly concave incline and drop-off into the big river. The symmetry and pure logic of those curves and angles, seen at a distance, take my breath away, always. The true shape of this great land is never so clear as along these mainly treeless places; every visual line, every wrinkle, is distinct, especially early in the day and late, when the sun angles low. The valley and canyon hang there in beauty and in time. The river sits unmoving, a muddy strip in its crack below, seeming to bulge with power.

There is illusion here of course, as usual. The truth is the canyon is in a state of constant, not even slow, motion. These arid benchlands, themselves composed of glacier- and meltwater-dropped clay silts, sand, gravels and the odd erratic, are much impacted by water, all forms of it: ice, snow, rainfall, seasonal runoffs, hailstorms, even vapour. Deluges happen. Lightning and thunder provide backup. Coulees, gulches, gullies and breaks erode and conform, providing shade or at least a more oblique angle from the sun so that moisture retention may occur. Plants—balsamroot sunflowers

Dry canyon country below Watson Bar. The two horizontal grooves across the hillside above the river are, respectively, an old wagon track and an older pack trail. Photo courtesy of Marne St. Claire.

and bunchgrass, and the occasional, usually solitary, Douglas fir or ponderosa pine—grow. There is much subtle ecological diversity here: zones and boundaries merging into each other; south slope and sun-facing north slope differences; low big-sage grasslands and canyon lands; higher-elevation parklands and fir forest; and visual differences—shapes and forms, textures and contrasts, sun, shadow, heights, depths, steeps, flats—each variation unique in the world, and all mesmerizing.

A way along, in an expanse of massive boulders on the downhill side, a blackened sod-roofed shack hunkers, a shrunken heat-soaked "soddy," going back to the old gold days, a haven for snakes no doubt, and built by somebody very short, obviously. There is no water in sight. Who had the temerity or desperation to live there, and why? This country has been short of rain for many years; the smaller creeks don't run, and groundwater-fed sloughs and potholes are drying.

Two or three miles farther, at a widening of the track, past a worn-out yellow Caterpillar with a yarding winch, a D6 or D7 I think, a small house trailer squats. Like the Cat, it is rust pocked and askew, and slowly sinking into the clay-dirt, its tires flat and rotten, its windows cracked and shot out, perished curtain fragments hanging limply. This trailer was clearly there for the duration—or until aluminum crumbles—somebody's quick dream, fore-shortened by the difficult road, or perhaps by lack of resolve.

Not far beyond the trailer, as a precursor to the main Lone Creek drainage beyond, Little Lone Creek flows. Creeks often seem to be named in pairs in this broad country: Churn, Gaspard, Dog, Graveyard, Paradise Creeks all have their "Little" equivalents located not far from them. There is a Little Churn Creek, a Little Gaspard, Little Graveyard, Little Paradise, and so on. Meason Creek, north of Dog Creek, was referred to in earlier times as Little Dog Creek. There is even a Little Big Bar Lake downstream from Big Bar Lake. It is as if the main creek was found and named, and then a significant branch or nearby parallel creek was later discovered, requiring a name that related it to the overall drainage system. The lesser Lone Creek in its little gully, fresh off the rimrock at the edge of the plateau above, its clear, cool water sparkling in the spring sun, was just naturally inviting. A few willows and water birches and small water-loving plants, acutely green, grow along its narrow edges. Close by where the creek runs over the road, what appears to be a roughly built, wooden confessional booth sits on its side, looking wildly misplaced; I pre-sume it was there as an aid to crossing at runoff time. And I wonder if modest Little Lone Creek will still be running by summer's end.

Beyond the creek, on a sloping flat above the road, standing as a kind of conclusion, and the source of the confessional, is a small, seemingly light blue church with a short, light blue steeple. Its blue seemed very clean, an extension of the sky on high, seen against the mountainside behind. But as moving cloud cover transforms the sky to grey, only bits of blue showing, the church turns grey also, and I realize its corrugated iron walls reflect whatever colour the sky happens to be. The old building has a patchy shake roof and a front porch disintegrated down to a few skeletal joists and posts on tight-stacked rocks above the wagon track, and is just the place for snakes, I would think.

Several diminutive, long-empty, squared-log houses, and barns not much more than sheds, cluster low and weather-worn behind mother church like a covey of obedient chicks. One building shows signs of having been used at least a little more recently; a pair of well-used work trousers, untouched in decades, hangs from a line, and a large, plain, cast iron cookstove, looking out of place, sits inside the door, askew, as if it had been left there temporarily. The buildings, all shapes and angles, all sun-blackened, look to be slowly subsiding into the sagebrush hillside. This place has been without people for a very long time.

The long-abandoned Roman Catholic church on its sloped bench at Lone Creek, looking truly alone. Photo courtesy of John Schreiber.

The situation reminds me of the old St'at'imc village site Nxo'isten, on the bench above the fishery at the mouth of Bridge River on the Fraser: the same blackened cabins crowded close to each other, the same long abandonment, the Catholic dream of a peaceful agrarian flock, the silent statement of trust. Only, at Bridge River the church is gone, the old houses and house sites, even at this late date, are more numerous, and the point overlooking the river is dominated by a densely populated cemetery full of old occupants and new—many of the former were short. The church had been a beauty, and I was fortunate to have seen it in the late 1960s, before either a brush fire or, according to repeated rumour, an arsonist, hurt and hateful I suppose, had burnt it out.

But this church at Little Lone Creek, with its back end into the hillside and its airy porch, is still standing after a century, unused but strong and

Cabins built a century ago, by and for aboriginal families, situated behind and above the church. Even semi-level places close to water in this narrow valley are scarce. Photo courtesy of John Schreiber.

clean looking, even from across the creek. I see no obvious signs of burial places. There must be a small cemetery up the hillside somewhere, perhaps on a point above the canyon.

I feel later, after wandering around and through it, that although the porch is dilapidated, the interior dusty, and the earth under the sagebrush and rabbitbush undisturbed, the building has a subtle sense of care and maintenance about it; it is so intact, so compact, so basically undefiled. Those few intruders that come by seem to have mostly come and gone.

Behind and above, the slopes are fairly gentle, in contrast to most of the rest of the valley. There is a lightly used trail heading up through the sage toward the timber: I don't follow it, though I am curious and would have liked to. "The horses found a back way in and out," Warren had said. I imagine this is such a way; another route would be from the north along the river. (A year later, Marne and I looked down on that church site from a tall basaltic bluff off the high trunk road and spotted game trails coming up out of the top of the sagebrush into the plateau timber above. At that same time, I spied two or three horses, just flecks of colour in the long, hot, hazy distance, grazing at the far end of the sloped flats by the old ranch next to Lone Creek. I could think of no reason why there might be domestic stock down there; those animals had to be wild. As I looked, they evaporated from sight, probably down into the creek bottom.)

I walk over and climb rather laboriously up onto the stonework foundations and shrunken joists of the porch into the church proper. Such a place deep in nowhere, such stillness, such a sense of no-time. The attention gone into its purpose, construction, use and sustained existence is palpable; you could breathe it. More than a hundred years of seasons have cultured it, preserved

The interior of the Lone Creek church. Photo courtesy of John Schreiber.

and settled it, given it authority of place and presence, all-pervading.

The nave is empty of pews; that which was easily removed is gone. But the paint is intact, the niches remain bracketing the three windows on either wall, and a striking raised altar still stands at the back of the chancel. The altar is imposing, its largeness modified by hand-carved filigree, not fine—coarse, in fact, but carefully and individually done, the various small asymmetries adding much to the overall liveliness. The ceiling where the nave and smaller chancel come together is made up of many carved battens, carefully fitted, each varying slightly to accommodate the different dimensions of the two sections of the building. There is a diminutive, shallow, choir balcony above the entrance beneath the short tower. On the ceiling of the chancel, at a central point, a small, painted, Roman Catholic heart, its detail clear but purpled with age, drips down upon us still for all who care to receive, and for those who don't.

Outside, on a bit of a bench, just past and above the church, sits a fairly modern brush-clearing machine. It's bright red and yellow, not especially rusted-out in this dry canyon climate; judging by the parts lying about, it broke down and was abandoned, but not before some attempts at monkey wrenching. That tough old sagebrush, gnarled and virtually indestructible, was too much for a mere piece of machinery. Lengths of unused irrigation pipe lie not far away. Uphill, a dried-out irrigation ditch curves down to where small fields had existed, the former pastures and hayfields of this exercise in faith, hope and agrarianism, slowly filling with sagebrush. There is still grass growing in patches close to the road, and the occasional pile of horse dung, some of it fresh. A row or two of fence line runs straight, posts and wire gone, with mature grey-green sage on one side and shorter, brighter new growth on the other, subtle variations in coloration and shading marking the difference. Mats of prickly pear cactus, the same as in the old western movies, but small and low, grow on the dry points. In early June they bloom, waxy exotic petals of the most glorious shades of peach-yellow. The warmth of the day has peaked.

I climb into my car for shade and to pause and rest before I drive on. My inclination is to take time to scan around me for a sense of this place, and to reflect on where I'm headed from here and how the day seems to be unfolding. The car windows are open to little breezes, refreshingly light on my face.

"My body and my land are the same."

The words of Chief Joseph Sinamulogh from the Lower Similkameen River country down south, part of a plea for a just settling of Indian land requirements in 1920, come again to mind: "My body and my land are the same."

I sit quietly. The high east-facing slopes are starting to darken. The day has cycled from shadow to sun-bleached high noon to the heat of the afternoon, and now shadows reach once again. Colours and shades, contours and shapes, contrasts, details, light, dark, are in slow, steady flux. Light wanes.

Even the light of the coming night, under a bright sky with a rising and falling moon, will change. Shadows will shift and move and disappear. After a while I start up the four-by-four and drive slowly away, my bedroll, clean T-shirts, maps and water in the back; my unnecessary raingear stowed away. I'm curious to see what I'll soon see. I navigate the last winding mile or two along the sagebrush river bench to Lone Creek and the little ranch buildings beside and above it. The air is cooling.

The ranch is an oasis in an arid land. The house is small and empty now, but it looks as if it had been well and carefully lived in and somehow protected by a pair of shade trees, acacias. It is a low Department of Indian Affairs type-home of fifties or sixties vintage, an intact building with a shiny metal roof. It has not been vacated for an unduly long time. A faded, whitewashed, single-pole fence, meant to discourage stock near the house but now partly fallen, runs across the front. A few outbuildings, some ancient, some merely old but intact, stand in behind. One, a substantial building of well-squared logs with neatly notched corners, includes a big, open room with a plywood floor—the original homestead house, no doubt. There is a small lean-to off it, for an electric light plant perhaps. A tall aerial pole for radio connections to the outside world stands firmly fixed to one corner. Everything seems neat; the area is largely clear of debris. A few fruit trees still grow and there are old signs of a long-worked kitchen garden. Somebody has tried to resurrect the garden space: there is recent digging and lengths of hose, fragments of rotten black-plastic sheeting and several remnants from last year's harvest, tall and stalky now, and gone to seed. The hot climate in the bottom of the canyon is suitable for a wide, even exotic, not to mention illicit, range of crops if you just add water. A grown-in irrigation ditch, fringed by a few stunted cottonwoods, curls out of the creek gully and along the edge of the hillside above the garden area. Lone Creek tumbles, its sound remote though it is just a short distance below, out of sight. A deep, strongly built, double-doored root cellar with good stonework walls is located on the dark side of the house. And on a corner of the northeast-facing porch by the front door, two fairly modern propane-gas stoves stand.

Ranch buildings at Lone Creek. Photo courtesy of John Schreiber.

Across the creek gully, on the slope opposite, an old wagon road slants up the sidehill north. Above it, even older, an original trail to gold runs, a small, determined, hand-dug slice out of the hillside. There are a couple of shallow kekuli holes between the back of the main house and the drop-off to the creek, plus two smaller circular depressions that look to have been old cooking or storage pits. There must surely be more kekulis somewhere around—on that high gravel bench on the sunny side of the creek mouth would be my guess.

By the creek below, on a little flat, are the remains of what must have been original buildings, two or three squared-log cabins, one precariously standing, the others just log ends and shreds of rotted fir now, but their shape and presence is clear. Wood must rot fast in the heavy creek-bottom air. There is a hay corral with scattered remnants of very old straw close by. Down the creek by the mouth, some distance away, is what looks like a sweathouse and a rough tent frame, a dry rack maybe, for salmon, and a defunct, flat-tired pickup, all moderately current. Might this have been an old salmon dipping place, a holdover from traditional days? I am tired enough not to walk down to check details.

A boneyard for old car bodies and farm machinery, offerings to the canyon, sits like a holy place on a point overlooking the river. One of the abandoned cars is a small, shiny, low-slung sedan, a fairly recent model, built for speed and utterly ill-fitted for this kind of country and road conditions, come to its rightful end here. A large sloping hayfield stretches south. Close by its near edge, late-afternoon sunlight refracts slightly off fresh horse shit.

My inclination, as always, is to go prowling for those old pithouses, but I am finished. I will go no farther today. I stand and gaze at the rock walls across the canyon and a broken old mining road low down in the steep talus, not going anywhere anymore. There would be wild sheep over there, pale, dry-belt California bighorns, including, once upon a time, a wild white sheep, an albino, so Warren Menhinick recounts. He said that because of its presence the herd across the river had been easy to spot. They are likely high up, out of sight, probably looking down at me right now, their protruding, goaty sheep eyes alert to any movement, witnessing the intrusion, missing nothing. That albino bighorn would be long dead and gone. I pause....

In the air: coolness, the river's murmur, a kestrel hunting, small breezes, meadowlark, pale grass waving, balm of Gilead creek-bottom smell, sun gold, the sanctity of silence. The day turns.

And I turn for a close last look at the house in the shade behind its white-washed railing. I peer in the big front window angled to the southeast. It seems as if the house had been situated for the absolute best view of all there was to see: the river, canyon walls, the broad sloped fields, livestock, hay crop, salmon-osprey-summer, deer to hunt, moving sheep on steep rock, geese winging south, snowline, changing weather, first green of spring, birds, the fence post where that meadowlark song sounds—distant figures, coyote trotting, looking back, an old man, all bent, alone, inevitable—too powerful an image to forget—Is that old Old Man I see come shuffling up the road? Transformer Old-One returning—the need is great

The room is large, mostly bare, dusty. Behind the glass, a man's lazy-boy chair sits, facing outward at an angle so as to include the room and the long view outside. The leg rest is up. The chair is covered in some kind of vinyl leatherette, cracked and worn. On the seat, placed square in the centre, a purple Bible sits as if planted, big, plainly and modestly bound, thoroughly thumbed. I picture an old man: stocky body, not fat, short iron-grey hair, hard dark hands, sitting there, in work jeans and suspenders; and an elderly woman with a life-worn face, creased, big-jointed hands, deep eyes, wearing a cotton print dress, maybe a cross round her neck, maybe a kerchief—a small crucifix hanging on the wall. Slowly, I incline my vision from the chair to across the canyon, slowly, and back, slowly.

Half certain, I stand in this place alone, body and mind quiet, mouth parted: there is a pause, a gentle letting go, a little breath fine as fine, a little intake in the heart—the place enters me. There is nothing to do here but surrender. Let what is be. We are not in charge.

WHEN I BEGAN TO WRITE THIS PIECE ON MY TIME AT LONE CREEK, SOME YEARS back, I found myself, one late evening, keyboarding each word by slow word, forming the phrases and sentences that would become the third paragraph on the opening page, the one about Lone Creek as a meditation. That series of slow-motion moments was a small epiphany: the words presenting themselves one by one, extended pauses after each, as if reluctant or unused to being here, but seemingly dictating themselves to me just the same. I was rapt; I barely breathed; it was as if the place Lone Creek was writing me. The whole formation took most of an hour.

I was and am still slow coming to know and acknowledge that places have a voice if we are still and quiet enough to listen down deep, and hear. To surrender to the pure truth of place is not always an easy or simple thing to do. Self obscures. Self reinvents time. Self finds every distracting crack. Self, being self-focused and short-sighted, seeks the illusion of management and control. Should you doubt that control is usually illusory, or at least ephemeral, just watch weather; note the unfolding of climates in their changing variations; observe a grizzly bear, a rat, your cat, a hawk high up, circling; spot the wilderness of your own old-aging. See yourself in a mirror. Take your time.

But letting go is utterly natural, especially if we do practise with some dedication, regularly and long-term. Spiritual practice in all its forms, meditation or prayer, for example, is a long sequence of surrenders. There may be nothing more basic to do in life than to surrender, and surrender again, in order to remember who and what and where we really are, and where we are going. In so doing we may learn to recognize and respect the primacy of great nature. We might see more clearly that we are each only a tiny part of great living nature, irrevocably connected; nothing more; nothing less. "Know thyself" the wise man said.

TWO SPRINGS AGO I REVISITED LONE CREEK. THE DRIVE IN WAS EASY ENOUGH; the ground was dry and hard, and the road seemed less narrow and daunting the second time in. I got there not long before dusk. The area around the ranch house was more rundown and dishevelled than before: garbage bits, a broken window, a plastic chair on its back in the yard—sure signs of passing careless use. A pair of flickers was pecking holes in a corner of a house wall. They flew off, protesting, as I stepped from the car.

I parked the Pathfinder on the edge of the track in front of the house. Later, in the depths of a good night's sleep, a small herd of horses came galloping close by the back end of my vehicle where I lay. I had the quick sense they were both curious and a bit unsettled by my unaccustomed human presence. There had been a group of six adults and a colt grazing in the far end of the big field when I first arrived. As I drove slowly along the road toward them, they faded down into the creek bottom in the usual manner, but not before one animal, a long-legged chestnut, looking as if he was the horse in charge, cantered out toward me, head up, tail and mane flying, putting on a show. He was checking to see what kind of a threat I might be and running interference, despite the distance between me and the herd.

In the early morning I went for a walk a mile or two farther north along the track on the sagebrush bench to see what I could see. The fresh hoofprints in the road dust were clear; there was not a shod horse in the bunch. The day was cool, the light was right, and I was able to spot the animals half-hidden in the edges of the fir forest some distance uphill from me: a dark speckled grey, a small black and white pinto, at least one sorrel and the big chestnut, all playing it safe and ready to run. I could see no sign of the young one or its mother. I was standing near a miner's low lean-to, open on three sides, as I watched them. The little structure was some hard-working man's summer shelter, going back to the dirty thirties, I surmise. Gold fetched a good price in those tough, hard-scrabble, desperate years, and the river would be running low.

Perhaps this coming spring, if I'm passing through and the road and rains allow, I will drive again down along the track to Lone Creek. I'll stand by the little ranch house with the big window for a while and wait and watch. The low sound of the creek and the still-inevitable lark's spring song will settle into me, and I'll listen. I will stay to hear the place if I'm able, if I'm allowed. There are some places around this country where time stops easily and connections naturally happen. Transformations occur.

When you find your place where you are,
practice occurs.

—Master Dogen

ACKNOWLEDGMENTS AND PHOTO CREDITS

AS ALWAYS, A HOST OF INDIVIDUALS HELPED ME IN THE WRITING OF *The Junction*. I'll begin by thanking all the generous folks and friends up-country: Van Andruss and Eleanor Wright from the Yalakom Valley, editors of *Lived Experience*; Earl and Jocelyn Cahill, Lawrence Joiner, Mike Brundage, and Don and Karen Logan, all from the Clinton area; Ria and Hennie Van Der Klis of Chilcotin Lodge at Riske Creek; Chilco Choate, still out there at Gaspard Lake; the great natural poet Lorne Dufour and Diana Geenson from up McLeese Lake way; Warren, Casie and Barry Menhinick, originally from Gold Bridge; Ken and Joy Schilling over at Darfield; Ordell Steen of the Friends of the Churn Creek Protected Area; and that not-so-grey eminence from Williams Lake, my very good friend Sage Birchwater. I am especially appreciative (and humbled) to know and work with Lillian Allison and Casey Sanders from Chopaka in the Lower Similkameen River country.

Closer to home, I express my gratitude for the friendly support of Don Brooks, long-time friend and hiking partner; his partner and wife, Dana Devine; Trevor Carolan; Theresa Kishkan; Robin and Jillian Ridington; Louise Smith; my old friends Gerry and Sharon Betts up at Port Alice; plus the usual Victoria crew— Tom Hueston, Trevor and Maureen Calkins, Bob Whittet, Peter Stein, Bruce Ruddell. As well, the enthusiastic voices of Stuart McLaughlin and Roseanna Means are audible all the way from Santa Fe, New Mexico. My thanks go out

Karen and Don Logan at Clinton. Photo courtesy of Marne St. Claire.

to you all. I owe a particular debt to Vici Johnstone, my publisher at Caitlin Press; Derek Fuller, my generous computer guru and friend next door; and Audrey McClellan, my astute, professional and patient editor. Thanks to Rolf Maurer at New Star Books for creating a map of the Churn Creek area, which we used as a resource for the map on page 12.

Here on the home front, there's my ever-expanding family to thankfully acknowledge, fine folks all of them: Bob and Mary Steele; my brothers, Chris and Andrew, and their spouses, Irene and Diane; Kirsten Kieferle out in Toronto; David, Samantha and newly arrived Oscar; Michael, Jenny and bright-eyed Svea; and Marne, whose caring support, intelligence, joy and love are a constant.

The photos in *The Junction* are excellent and I am especially proud to have had access to all of them. Marne is the photographer of most. Other crucial contributors are Don Logan, who kindly supplied me copies of old photos from his extensive South Cariboo history collection, and my brother Chris Schreiber. Earl Cahill is responsible for the spectacular frontispiece photo, and Chris Harris of Country Light Publishing, Damon West of Damon West Photography,

Larry Travis of Raincoast Images and Chris Genovali and Jane Woodland of Raincoast Conservation Foundation have all generously allowed me the use of several outstanding animal photographs.

I've been blessed by the kindness of many. If there are mistakes here, I made them.

I wish to acknowledge, as well, all those responsible for the creation and maintenance of the Churn Creek Protected Area at Empire Valley and up Churn Creek, and Junction [bighorn] Sheep Range Provincial Park between the Fraser and lower Chilcotin Rivers. These places are of immense ecological value to the webs of life in the British Columbia Interior, and

Marne St. Claire at Writing-on-Stone. Photo courtesy of Marne St. Claire and John Schreiber.

to all of us who value wild life, wild places and ecological diversity. May California bighorn sheep continue to survive and flourish.

I had originally intended to include an essay honouring three individuals who are essential to my understanding of backcountry and wilderness. Instead, I'll simply acknowledge them briefly now: Gary Snyder, great poet, essayist, woodsman, practising Zen Buddhist, exemplar and long-time voice for wilderness; anthropologist Robin Ridington, whose writings so elegantly and wisely explore the subtle survival world of the early-contact, shamanistic Dane-zaa hunting people of northeast BC. Those old hunting and gathering folks are some of our spiritual ancestors, and among them, in Robin's time, were the last of the old-time dreamers, certain old hunters whose dreaming was fundamental to successful hunting, survival and a good life.

Last, I'm glad to acknowledge Pat Schreiber, fine woodsman, hunter, fisherman, logger, gentleman, lover of the wild, and father to my brothers, Chris and Andrew, and me. With his woods skills, knowledge and intelligent curiosity, developed out of necessity in his own childhood, and with the backup of our mother, Alizon, Dad demonstrated the practice and art of living in wild places in an observant and respectful manner. Life on the edge of the bush was usually fun and always interesting with Pat in the lead. We were fortunate young lads. As Andrew exclaimed the other month, "They don't make 'em like that anymore."

> *The Pygathoreans used to marvel*
> *when they met with*
> *a city-bred man who had never seen a*
> *divine being.*
> —Testimonia of Apuleius
> quoted by John Murray in "Wolf Country"
> in *Out Among the Wolves*

RESOURCES AND FURTHER READING

Anthropology/Archaeology/Mythology

Archaeological Society of Alberta, Project 20. *Story on Stone: A Photographic Record of Rock Art in the Southern Alberta Area Surrounding the City of Lethbridge*. Lethbridge: Archaeological Society of Alberta Lethbridge Centre, 1980.

Bierhorst, John. *The Mythology of North America*. New York: William Morrow, 1985.

Boas, Franz. Introduction to *Traditions of the Thompson River Indians of British Columbia*, by James Teit. New York: Kraus Reprint Co., 1969. First published 1898 by Houghton Mifflin.

Bouchard, Randy, and Dorothy Kennedy, eds. *Lillooet Stories*. Sound Heritage vol. 6, no. 1. Victoria: Provincial Archives of British Columbia, 1977.

Bringhurst, Robert. "The Meaning of Mythology." In *Everywhere Being is Dancing*. Kentville, NS: Gaspereau, 2007.

Bryan, Liz. *The Buffalo People*. Edmonton: University of Alberta Press, 1991.

Campbell, Joseph. *Historical Atlas of World Mythology*. Vol. 1: *The Way of the Animal Powers*, Parts 1 and 2. New York: Harper and Row, 1988.

Corner, John. *Pictographs in the Interior of British Columbia*. Self-published, 1968.

Dormaar, Johan. *Sweetgrass Hills*. Lethbridge: Lethbridge Historical Society, 2005.

Duff, Wilson. *The Indian History of British Columbia*. Victoria: BC Provincial Museum, 1964.

———. "The World Is as Sharp as a Knife: Meaning in Northwest Coast Art." In *The World Is as Sharp as a Knife*, ed. Donald Abbott. Victoria: BC Provincial Museum, 1981.

Glavin, Terry. *Nemiah: The Unconquered Country*. Vancouver: New Star, 1992.

Halifax, Joan. *Shaman*. London: Thames and Hudson, 1982.

Harner, Michael. *The Way of the Shaman*. New York: Harper and Row, 1980.

Hayden, Brian, ed. *A Complex Culture of the British Columbia Plateau*. Vancouver: UBC Press, 1992.

Hultkrantz, Ake. *The Religions of the American Indians*. Berkeley: University of California Press, 1967.

Josephy, Alvin M., Jr. *The Nez Perce Indians*. Lincoln: University of Nebraska Press, 1965.

Kerenyi, Karl. "The Trickster in Relation to Greek Mythology." In *The Trickster: A Study in American Indian Mythology*, by Paul Radin. New York: Schocken, 1972.

Lewis-Williams, David. *The Mind in the Cave*. London: Thames and Hudson, 2002.

Lopez, Barry. *Giving Birth to Thunder, Sleeping with His Daughter*. New York: Avon, 1977.

Maud, Ralph, ed. *The Salish People: The Local Contributions of Charles Hill-Tout*. Vol. 1: *The Thompson and the Okanagan*. Vancouver: Talon, 1978.

———. *A Guide to B.C. Indian Myth and Legend*. Vancouver: Talon, 1982.

Neihardt, John G. *Black Elk Speaks*. Lincoln: University of Nebraska Press, 1961.

Nelson, Richard. *Make Prayers to the Raven*. Chicago: University of Chicago Press, 1983.

Radin, Paul. *The Trickster*. New York: Schocken, 1972.

Ridington, Robin. "The Inner Eye of Shamanism and Totemism." In *Teachings from the American Earth*, ed. Dennis and Barbara Tedlock. New York: Liveright, 1975.

———. *Little Bit Know Something*. Vancouver: Douglas and McIntyre, 1990.

Ridington, Robin, and Jillian Ridington. *Where Happiness Dwells*. Vancouver: UBC Press, 2013.

Robinson, Harry. *Write It on Your Heart*. Compiled and edited by Wendy Wickwire. Vancouver: Talon, 1989.

Snyder, Gary. "The Incredible Survival of Coyote." In *The Old Ways*. San Francisco: City Lights, 1977.

Teit, James. *The Lillooet Indians*. Vol. 2, part 5, Publications of the Jesup North Pacific Expedition, ed. Franz Boas. New York: AMS Press, 1975. First published 1906 by G.E. Stechert.

———. *The Shuswap*. Vol. 2, part 7, Publications of the Jesup North Pacific Expedition, ed. Franz Boas. New York: AMS Press, 1975. First published 1909 by G.E. Stechert.

———. *The Thompson Indians of British Columbia*. Vol.1, part 4, Publications of the Jesup North Pacific Expedition, ed. Franz Boas. New York: AMS Press, 1975. First published 1900 in New York.

———. *Traditions of the Thompson River Indians of British Columbia*. New York: Kraus Reprint Co., 1969. First published 1898 by Houghton Mifflin.

———. *The Okanagon*. In *The Salishan Tribes of the Western Plateaus* (Forty-fifth Annual Report of the Bureau of American Ethnology to the Secretary of the Smithsonian Institution, 1927–28), edited by Franz Boas, 198–294. Seattle: The Shorey Book Store. First published 1930 by the US Government Printing Office.

York, Annie, Richard Daly, and Chris Arnett. *They Write Their Dreams on the Rock Forever*. Vancouver: Talon, 1993.

British Columbia History

Beeson, Edith. *Dunlevy: From the Diaries of Alex P. McInnes*. Lillooet: Lillooet Publishers, 1971.

Belyk, Robert C. *John Tod: Rebel in the Ranks*. Victoria: Horsdal and Schubart, 1995.

Blacklaws, Rick, and Diana French. *Ranchland*. Madeira Park, BC: Harbour, 2001.

Cox, Doug. *Ranching: Now, Then, and Way Back When...* Penticton: Skookum Publications, 2004.

Laing, F.W. "Some Pioneers of the Cattle Industry." Photocopy of an article from *British Columbia Historical Quarterly* 6, October 1942.

M'Gonigle, Michael, and Wendy Wickwire. *Stein: The Way of the River*. Vancouver: Talon, 1988.

Morice, A.G. *The History of the Northern Interior of British Columbia*. Smithers, BC: Interior Stationery, 1978. First published 1904.

Reksten, Terry. *The Illustrated History of British Columbia*. Vancouver: Douglas and McIntyre, 2001.

Rothenburger, Mel. *The Wild McLeans*. Victoria: Orca, 1993.

Veillette, John, and Gary White. *Early Indian Village Churches*. Vancouver: UBC Press, 1977.
Ware, Reuben. *Five Issues Five Battlegrounds*. Chilliwack, BC: Coqualeetza Education Training Centre, 1983.

Local History: Cariboo–Chilcotin

Andrews, Gerry. *Big Bar Country*. Self-published, 1995.
BC Parks. Cariboo District. *Churn Creek Protected Area Management Plan*. Victoria: Ministry of Environment, Lands and Parks, BC Parks Division, 2000.
Drinkell, A.J. *Address before the Cariboo Historical Society*. [Williams Lake], 1950.
Good Earth Parks. *Great Canadian Parks: Churn Creek* [video]. Toronto: Good Earth Productions,1999.
Harris, Bob. "Tsoloss Ridge: South of Nemaia Valley." *B.C. Outdoors*, October 1975.
———. "Tchaikazan-Yohetta." *B.C. Outdoors*, 1983.
Knezevich, Fred. "Empire Valley Ranch." 1996. Photocopy of a paper in the Williams Lake Museum.
Koster, Henry. "A Brief History of the Empire Valley Ranch." n.d. Photocopy of a paper in the Clinton Museum, courtesy of Mike Brundage.
Logan, Don. *Pioneer Pictures of Big Bar Mountain*. Victoria: Trafford, 2005.
———. *Dog Creek: 100 years*. Victoria: Trafford, 2007.
———. *Thaddeus Harper*. Self-published, 2008.
———. *Canoe Creek BC*. Self-published, 2011.
Marriott, Harry. *Cariboo Cowboy*. Victoria: Gray's, 1966.
Orchard, Imbert, interviewer. *Tales of the Ranches*. People in Landscape Series. Victoria: Provincial Archives of British Columbia, 1964.
Patenaude, Branwen. *Trails to Gold*. Victoria: Horsdal and Schubart, 1995.
Place, Hilary. *Dog Creek*. Surrey, BC: Heritage House, 1999.
Ricker, Karl. "Mt. Tatlow: An Access Trick." *Canadian Alpine Journal* 66, 1983.
———. "Tchaikazan Valley Earth Science Notes." *Canadian Alpine Journal* 59, 1976.
Schreiber, John. *Old Lives: In the Chilcotin Backcountry*. Halfmoon Bay, BC: Caitlin, 2011.
———. *Stranger Wycott's Place*. Transmontanus 17. Vancouver: New Star, 2008.
St. Pierre, Paul. *Chilcotin Holiday*. Vancouver: Douglas and McIntyre, 1984.
Stangoe, Irene. *Cariboo-Chilcotin, Pioneer People and Places*, Surrey BC: Heritage House, 1994.
Tatla Lake School Heritage Project. *Hoofprints in History*. Vol. 3. Tatla Lake, BC: Tatla Lake Elementary Junior Secondary School, 1986–2000.
Witte Sisters [Veera Bonner]. *Chilcotin: Preserving Pioneer Memories*. Surrey, BC: Heritage House, 1995.
Wyborn, M., and G. Barford. "Tchaikazan Valley ACC Vancouver Section Camp 1-14 August 1982." *Canadian Alpine Journal* 66, 1983.

Local History: Similkameen/Okanagan

Barlee, N.L. *Gold Creeks and Ghost Towns*. Surrey, BC: Hancock House, 1993.
———. *Gold Creeks and Ghost Towns of Northeastern Washington*. Surrey, BC: Hancock House, 1988.
———. *Similkameen: The Pictograph Country*. Surrey, BC: Hancock House, 1989.
Grainger, M. Allerdale. *Riding the Skyline*. Victoria: Horsdal and Schubert, 1994.
Harris, Bob. "The 1848 HBC Trail," "The Hope Trail," and "The West Bank Trail." In *The Best of B.C.'s Hiking Trails*. Vancouver: Maclean Hunter, 1986.
Harris, R.C., and H. Hatfield. "Old Pack Trails in the Proposed Cascade Wilderness." Summerland, BC: Okanagan Similkameen Parks Society, 1980.
Ormsby, Margaret A., ed. *A Pioneer Gentlewoman in British Columbia*. Vancouver: UBC Press, 1976.
Rhenisch, Harold. *Out of the Interior*. Vancouver: Cacanadadada, 1993.

Natural History

Ackerman, Jennifer. "Cranes." *National Geographic Magazine*, April 2004.
Campbell, Wayne, Neil K. Dawe, Ian McTaggart-Cowan, John M. Cooper, Gary W. Kaiser, and Michael C.E. McNall. *The Birds of British Columbia*. Vol. 2. Victoria: Royal BC Museum, 1990.
Cannings, Richard, and Sydney Cannings. *British Columbia: A Natural History*. Vancouver: Greystone, 1996.
Harris, Chris. *Spirit in the Grass*. 105 Mile Ranch: Country Life, 2007.
Hatler, David, David Nagorsen, and Alison Beal. *Carnivores of British Columbia*. Victoria: Royal BC Museum, 2008.
Lyons, C.P., and W. Merilees. *Trees, Shrubs and Flowers to Know in British Columbia and Washington*. Vancouver: Lone Pine, 1995.
Matthiessen, Peter. *The Birds of Heaven*. Vancouver: Greystone, 2001.
McTaggart-Cowan, Ian, and C.J. Guiget. *Mammals of British Columbia*. Victoria: BC Provincial Museum, n.d.
Murie, Olaus. *A Field Guide to Animal Tracks*. Boston: Houghton Mifflin, 1954.
National Geographic. *Birds of North America*. Washington, DC: National Geographic Society, 1983.
Parish, R., R. Coupe, and D. Lloyd. *Plants of Southern Interior British Columbia*. Vancouver: Lone Pine, 1996.
Shackleton, David. *Hoofed Mammals of British Columbia*, Vancouver: UBC Press, 1999.
Stebbins, Robert C. *A Field Guide to Western Reptiles and Amphibians*. Boston: Houghton Mifflin, 1966.
Turner, Nancy J. *Food Plants of British Columbia Indians*. Part 2: *Interior People*. Victoria: Royal BC Museum, 1978.

Turner, Nancy, Randy Bouchard, and Dorothy I.D. Kennedy. *Ethnobotany of the Okanagan-Colville Indians of British Columbia and Washington*. Victoria: BC Provincial Museum, 1980.
White, Gordon R. *Stein Valley: Wilderness Guidebook*. Vancouver: Stein Wilderness Alliance, 1991.

General Reading or Viewing

Aitken, Robert. "Gandhi, Dogen and Deep Ecology." In *The Mind of Clover*. San Francisco: North Point, 1984.
Barry, P.S. *Mystical Themes in Milk River Art*. Edmonton: University of Alberta Press, 1991.
Davis, Wade. *Into the Silence*. Toronto: Vintage Canada, 2012.
Dogen, Eihei. "The Mountains and Rivers Sutra." In *The Mountain Spirit*, ed. Michael Tobias and Harold Drasdo. Woodstock, NY: Overlook, 1979.
LaChapelle, Dolores. *Earth Wisdom*. Silverton, CO: Finn Hill Arts, 1978.
Martel, Jan-Marie. *Bowl of Bone: Tale of the Syuwe* [video]. Vancouver: Turtle Production, 1993.
Matthiessen, Peter. *Lost Man's River* [video]. New York: Mystic Fire Video, 1990.
———. *Nine-Headed Dragon River*. Boston: Shambhala, 1985.
McCart, Joyce and Peter. *On the Road with David Thompson*. Calgary: Fifth House, 2000.
Murray, John, ed. *Out Among the Wolves*. Vancouver: Whitecap Books, 1993.
Raban, Jonathan. *Bad Land*. New York: Vintage, 1996.
Rodegast, Pat, and Judith Stanton. *Emmanuel's Book II: The Choice for Love*. New York: Bantam, 1989.
Snyder, Gary. "Blue Mountains are Constantly Walking." In *The Practice of the Wild*. San Francisco: North Point, 1990.
———. *The Practice of the Wild*. San Francisco: North Point, 1990.
———. "The Wilderness." In *Turtle Island*. New York: New Directions, 1974.
Snyder, Gary, and Jim Harrison. *The Etiquette of Freedom*. Berkeley: Counterpoint, 2010.
Steinbeck, John. *Cannery Row*. In *Of Mice and Men and Cannery Row*. New York: Penguin, 1945.

JOHN SCHREIBER GREW UP IN COASTAL LOGGING communities and—for five formative, young years—in the North Thompson Valley north of Kamloops. He has worked extensively in the logging industry, in a mining camp, on a seine fishboat, in a pulp mill, as a parole officer and as a teacher-counselor for 27 years. Since the late '60s he has walked, driven and ridden through the Chilcotin region many times. Now retired, he lives in Victoria with his partner, Marne. His earlier collections of stories from the Chilcotin include *Old Lives: In the Chilcotin Backcountry* (Caitlin Press, 2011) and *Stranger Wycott's Place* (New Star Books, 2008).